Improving
America's
Schools

IMPROVING AMERICA'S SCHOOLS

Bruce Joyce
Booksend Laboratories

Longman
New York & London

Executive Editor: Raymond O'Connell
Developmental Editor: Naomi Silverman
Cover Design: Nina Tallarico
Compositor: Times Printing Inc.
Printer and Binder: Haddon Craftsmen, Inc.

Improving America's Schools

Library of Congress Cataloging in Publication Data

Joyce, Bruce R.
  Improving America's schools.

  Bibliography: p.
  Includes index.
  1. Education—United States—Aims and objectives.
2. Educational planning—United States. 3. Education
and state—United States. I. Title.
LA217.J69   1985   370'.973   85-233
ISBN 0-582-28580-1

85 86 87 88 9 8 7 6 5 4 3 2 1

To Beverly Showers

Contents

Preface

Our schools are a bit Candide-like. Ingenuous, they are tossed about in the ocean of our culture. Rudderless at times, they tenaciously cling to their role as the mediators of learning. They are conservative in tenor, for they are supposed to anchor our heritage. Yet they must prepare students for contemporary life and teach them to live with social currents and technological developments yet unimagined.

It is clear that schools must be congenial to sensible change if they are to do their job properly. They must continuously blend new knowledge and processes with the old, discarding the obsolete and ensuring that the new mix is powerful and humane.

Today the challenge of school improvement is arresting. For years there has been too little concern with continuing the education of teachers and administrators. Research has given us powerful tools that are underused—even unknown to many. The real task of school improvement is not just to bring specific innovations into play, but to unite community members, teachers, and administrators in the development of an environment where the continuous improvement of education is normal.

Bruce Joyce

Improving America's Schools

Introduction

ENERGY FOR EXCELLENCE

As Lawrence Cremin (1965) put it so very well, the "genius" of American education is the establishment of the common school. Politically, it is an amazing achievement, because the Constitution did not mention education, so there was no central ministry of education with the authority to develop an educational system. The citizens of the new states and the territories not yet states had to find the energy to create schools. These states did not establish central agencies with the executive authority to organize education. Rather, communities established the local education authorities that we call school districts. Currently there are more than 17,000 of them. Some are massive (the New York City board of education employs more than 60,000 teachers). Others represent tiny hamlets. Altogether, more than 85,000 school board members labor to govern these districts that employ a total of more than two million teachers and nearly a million additional personnel, including cafeteria workers and bus drivers. Forty million children are housed daily in our schools.

The goal has been to provide a basic and rigorous education for all and the opportunity for vocational and talent development to the extent of each person's abilities and motivation. It took a long time to reach the point where our schools were providing a basic education for most of our citizens. In 1900, the average person received only 7 years of schooling and nearly 20% never attended school at all. Not until shortly before World War II did half of our population graduate from high school, and only about

10% of these graduates received higher education. Only after World War II did the system expand to its present state, where nearly everyone attends school and more than half obtain some higher education. Along the way our developing system had to contend with many of the problems that are embedded in our social structure. It has been difficult to provide adequate education to the concentrations of economically poor people in some of our cities and rural areas. The poor have fewer resources to put into education, their children have fewer educationally related advantages at home, it is more difficult to attract talented administrators and teachers to poor areas, and the conditions of life in those areas can be trying. Differences in sex roles have been reflected in the educational system as well. Currently, however, more females graduate from high school than males and about an equal number attend colleges. Racial and ethnic divisions have continued to result in segregated education for many, and black and hispanic students still have great educational disadvantages. Children with physical, emotional, and intellectual handicaps often have become outsiders to the system, although during the last 10 years great efforts have been made to provide for special needs. Also, persons with obvious intellectual and artistic attainments often have struggled to find a challenging education at the elementary and secondary levels, although the university system is now vast and offers a great variety of opportunities for the talented and motivated.

The state governments have taken active roles in promoting minimal standards for schools, and the federal government and some states have been active in providing resources to try to reduce inequities in educational opportunities. The federal government has provided limited amounts of money for educational research and development, although the amounts have declined substantially in recent years, to about one fourth of their level in the early seventies.

Can we call the results of our efforts an educational system?

The answer is that it depends on how you look at it. Let us apply three criteria. (1) A system should utilize procedures that represent the best practice known to the field; (2) it should have the capability to improve itself and to adapt procedures to changing conditions, and (3) a close relationship should exist between policy and operations.

If we ask the question, how similar (or different) are teaching and curriculum practices in the nation's public schools, the answer is that they are remarkably similar across the nation. The topics taught in the various grades are quite predictable from state to state and between districts. Wealthier communities have a somewhat richer variety of offerings, and the big schools can offer more electives than can small ones, but the three R's dominate the primary grades everywhere and the standard subjects—English, social studies, science, and mathematics—are taught in all of the high schools.

The textbook defines the content in the vast majority of classrooms everywhere. Most homework assignments are taken from textbooks and workbooks. Most instruction consists of recitations of and discussions about material from the textbooks. Although there are some differences among textbooks produced for classroom use, in most subject areas they are more similar than different.

Testing programs also are relatively standardized. A half-dozen test makers supply the tests that are used in most of the nation's schools and the results are reported in "national norms" so that every child, classroom, school, and district can be compared to every other one. Increasingly, these tests have influenced the curriculum because they have become the standard by which the success of the schools is judged. The College Board examinations are powerful influences on secondary curriculums.

If we ask the question, "Do the procedures used represent the best practice available?", we have a decidedly mixed picture. The common textbook-oriented recitations and discussions are fine for some purposes, but there is a large storehouse of tested curriculums, technologies, and teaching methods that are seldom used but which do get results if they are used properly.

Do schools have the capability to improve themselves? The answer is that schools vary widely, but most have very limited capability. Obviously, without a central educational authority, there is no governance structure for deciding on nationwide directions for school improvement. State departments of education are loosely connected to the schools and can enforce minimum standards but not excellence. Even many school district offices are not tightly connected to the operation of the schools.

A critical factor is that in most districts very little time is built into the teaching job for teachers to learn new curriculums and teaching techniques. Thus, a curriculum change is very difficult to implement and teachers are virtually unable to get training in new teaching techniques and technologies. As a result, many powerful programs are virtually unused in today's schools, simply because the system does not provide the means for its personnel to learn them.

Is there a close relationship between policy and operations? The answer is that a much closer relationship exists when the logistics of the operation are involved—food services, transportation, and the procurement of instructional supplies—than in the programmatic areas where curriculum and instruction are involved. Partly this is because many school administrators are oriented toward logistics and community relations and are little interested in instructional leadership. Many confess that they are not competent to lead their faculties in updating curriculum and instruction, even if the time for staff training were available to them. Without interested and competent leadership and strong staff development programs, policy for educational substance and process will not be articulated into action.

We have a situation where operations over the nation have become relatively standardized and are maintained through textbook production and testing procedures. Yet, the connection between local administrators and operations is tenuous in many cases, so that the adaptaion of procedures to local conditions is difficult and policy-related school improvement is arduous. And, finally, the lack of investment in staff development virtually precludes major changes or improvements.

The effect is that under the present organization the current operation of the schools can be maintained relatively well, but defects are difficult to remedy and promising practices are hard to implement. Over the last 20 years careful research has documented that the current school organization is not congenial to curriculum changes or to the introduction of educational technologies or to new ways of utilizing personnel. Hence, the old schoolhouse is getting sadly out of date and we need to create the means for doing something about it.

We need to do this because we have almost reached consensus that American education must be improved. "National" reports follow one another and either proclaim virtual emergencies (National Commission on Excellence in Education, 1984) or soberly question the adequacy of the current structure of schools (Goodlad, 1983) or the intellectual substance of its curriculum (Sizer, 1984). Its flexibility to reach the poor or children of special needs is still seriously questioned and the black and hispanic populations still appear to be seriously disadvantaged in its environment. Increasing numbers of families are turning, at great cost, to private schools and academies, because they do not have confidence in our public system of education.

Until recently it reasonably could be thought that the obvious defects of the American system were well worth the price of a common education. We did not pretend that our common school could provide the intellectual drive of nations who only educated an elite, or who ruthlessly eliminated at an early age those who are slow to mature. We did believe, however, our schools could provide a common education with a rich variety of channels, so that talent could be developed to a high degree. Our world leadership in so many technologies, arts, and athletics seemed to justify our belief.

The launching of Sputnik gave us pause for thought, as has the rapid rise of technical development in other nations.

One underlying assumption in this book is that it is now clear that some other nations that also developed common schools are generating levels of achievement for *all* their children — not just for those of obviously high native talent or privileged family background — that far exceed those of our own. One of America's most careful researchers has recently conducted investigations in Japan in which he has given American achievement tests in mathematics to Japanese children. By the 6th grade, all of the Japanese children (including their "slow" learners) are equaling or exceeding the achievement of our best students (Walberg, 1985). Evidence like this challenges the notion that it is inevitable that a common school system will have to be satisfied with achievement at the levels we have tolerated. Moreover, the Japanese built their system in a relatively short time — only 40 years.

When information like this comes to the attention of American citizens and educators, the first reactions are frequently, "But, doesn't the high achievement result in high suicide rates?" and "Isn't it due to the family and the family attitudes toward learning?" The answer to the first question is no. A number of Western countries have higher adolescent suicide rates, and in the United States the rate has been rising while achievement apparently has been declining. To answer the second question, it must be acknowledged that families do influence achievement. However, so do schools. Japanese schools promote more self-study, including study after hours, and more complex learning tasks. The task of the school is to create an educational program that works. If another country can develop an educational system that powerfully reaches all children, then so can we. Schools can be very powerful, and they can work with families in partnerships so that each benefits from the other.

Another assumption that propels this book is that we must get down to the business of creating more powerful and more joyful schools. How we might go about it and what those schools might look like is the subject we will explore. Because we have a system based on local governance of education, a great many of us we will need to be involved in school improvement. We have to raise our sights and have confidence that we can revitalize our massive system, producing a level of excellence in our smallest school that is beyond the level of our best ones now.

In Part I, I will explore common ideas about our schools and the problem of building cooperative school improvement programs. In Part II, I will look at one model of a school for the future, based on contemporary educational research and develop-ment, and will use it to stretch our imaginations. In Part III, I will examine a program for school improvement based on recent research about educational change.

There are no easy solutions to the problems that face schools. There are straightforward ways to improve them, however, if we have the energy and resolve to use them.

I

REALISTIC IDEALISM

1

Social Purpose
and Education

This book is classically American in the down-home, fundamental sense of the term. Its ideas reflect our style, the idealistic side of our heritage, and our contradictory urges to change and yet remain the same. It is built on the outrageous assumption that, when necessary, we can study, modify, and even radically change a social institution, despite habit and tradition. This innate optimism directly challenges what we know about the difficulties of cultural change and our past failure to bring about lasting innovations in curriculum and teaching. Although they have been sharpened by some very recent research, the ideas presented in this book are not new. They are just a blend of the ideas and beliefs that Americans have produced over the past two centuries as we have sought powerful and humane education to preserve our society and free the energy of our children to make it better. This spirit was clearly expressed by John Dewey, who understood that the existence of democracy depends on educating ourselves for it — that education makes a differnce in the conduct of social and personal life and must reflect our ideals rather than our anxieties (Dewey, 1918).

   Also typically American is our belief that the schools belong to the people, an ownership that finds its most powerful expression in the local community. Americans have not delegated the control of education to a "central ministry of education" that can be depended on to maintain a high quality school system and ensure its continuous improvement. The reciprocal of this belief is that local citizens have an obligation to become active and thoughtful participants in the overall governance of their schools and in the educational process within them. The home, the school, and the student must march together.

We believe in strength through diversity, expressed around a common cultural core. We do not fear social division along cultural lines but reaffirm the tradition that seeks to draw the best from all our heritages and to integrate them for the common good. Cultural differences enhance us, they do not endanger us. We are distressed by the glassy homogeneity of our schools and think we can express our diversity in educational alternatives that lie within the common ground of our heritage. We believe we are committed and flexible enough to embrace variety and be strengthened by it.

Our belief in planning is another part of our idealistic heritage. Part of our vision is that vigorous local planning prevents domination by any central core, however wise and benevolent. Planning is our unique style, the expression of our pragmatism. We do not like to leave things to chance but believe that we can select intelligent goals and find efficient means of achieving them. Our resistance to habitual automatic solutions to problems is based on our belief that we can create options that lie beyond the reach of present practice.

We also recognize that we can be our own worst enemies in the battle for effective schools, that habit and traditional practice can become so ingrained that they threaten to submerge any innovation, however sensibly it is presented. Implementation of even small improvements is difficult and requires intensive effort.

Although we often are accused of being excessively pragmatic, of being interested only in the most efficient means to immediate goals, we have an abiding love of knowledge and a belief that education enhances the quality of human existence. Our society has a love - hate relationship with intellectuals that alternates between a suspicion of the "ivory tower" and a near-reverence for the scholarly. The tie is inescapable, however: schooling is the channel not only to advanced inquiry and higher knowledge, but to a balanced understanding of the role of scholarly knowledge in the life of everyone. What is central is the love of learning — the act of reaching beyond our present conceptions.

A corollary is our appreciation of talent, our understanding that interesting minds bring us new creations, new understandings, and richer aspirations. Along with that, we have an appreciation of the handicapped — a belief that all children have the talent and the right to live productive lives.

We believe in teachers and refuse to be intimidated by talk of burnout and retrenchment. We value the lives of teachers — both for their own sake and because the lives of our children depend so much on the growth of their mentors. We also have learned that we must greatly increase teachers' initial and continuing education. We must take responsibility for the academic and clinical competence of teachers.

All of this leads those of us who labor in education to continue our struggle to make schools more effective. We believe that we already possess a rich heritage of alternative models of curriculum and teaching and that we can become not only better users of them but the inventors of new ones as well. In short, we are infected with the "can do" attitude of the cockeyed optimist.

During the past 15 years we have listened to many harsh words about the state of public education. The penchant of the media for hyperbole has at times created a mood of near hysteria about our schools, has blamed them for declining worker productivity, changes in moral standards, presumed growing illiteracy and drops in academic standards, the failure of industries to stand up to foreign competition, and crime in the cities. We live in an age of exaggeration, where the evening news is divided between the local murder report, the national corruption report, and the international war report, and, interspersed, we have the "schools are going to the dogs" report and a few other brief reports purportedly documenting the imminent demise of our social institutions. Generally, the reports end with the implication that there is either an evil force or an incompetent bureaucrat behind the problem, and that a sheer act of will can clean up the situation.

Treating just our little corner of the social scene — the school — we wish to provide an antidote. School staffs contain mostly plain hard-working citizens usually unafflicted by extremes of ignorance, irresponsibility, or sadism. Yet, if we reasonably and thoughtfully examine the health of our schools, we will learn that they can be made much more powerful than they are, not because they have declined over the years, but because in this changing world, our economic troubles, coupled with negative publicity, have depressed our investment in our schools and retarded their modernization. In this rapidly changing world the demands of changing populations strain our traditional ways of organizing schools, while technological developments offer fabulous possibilities that the schools of yesterday could not have imagined. In other words, because we have organized education as we have, we must all accept responsibility for our schools and for their improvement. This will not be easy, for more powerful ways of educating are rapidly developing — ways with which few citizens, teachers, and school administrators are acquainted.

Also — we have to face the fact that for the first time there is clear evidence that some other societies are surpassing us in the management of education. We have been complacent. We have not challenged ourselves as we should. To reach all our population we will have to change the nature of our public dialogue about education and begin to conduct schools in new ways.

2

A Matter of Resolve

The headlines are strident. The titles of reports (*A Nation at Risk*) smack of doomsday. A series of presidents of very different social persuasions warn the public that the condition of schools threatens the social order and the talents of our children. The message is clear. The American people have lost confidence in their schools. The huge common school complex is in the same public-relations boat as the post office and the passenger train. However, the crisis of confidence in the schoolhouse is much more serious than the loss of faith in the letterbox and the locomotive. Delayed letters are annoying but not devastating. The car and the airplane stepped in when train schedules diminished. But to believe that our schools are failing is to believe also that our future as a healthy society is precarious. The thought that 40 million children currently are receiving a poor education gives rise to a near panic.

To make things worse, the current crisis in world trade and military competition produces a nagging fear that our schools have been in bad shape for quite a long time. As Americans watch an overcrowded island nation that must import nearly all of its fossil fuels overwhelm our automobile and electronics industries, the inevitable conclusion is that the "good old days" in American education were not so good after all —they simply planted a time

13

bomb that is now exploding as our managers and workers sink under the confident and orderly onslaught of the Mitsubishis and Sonys. Japan, regarded as a rigidly backward-looking and imitative nation until the time of World War II, now voluntarily cuts back exports to relieve the pressure on American industries. Arabian sheiks, perceived as medieval only a generation ago, toy with American bankers and transnational corporations. Russians, ridiculed as feudal only a hundred years ago, calmly force American foreign policy strategists into reaction and repeatedly demonstrate greater knowledge of Third World nations. And all the while, our great cities crumble with physical decay and social strife. But, at the same time, the power of the American experiment broods beneath the indignity. The nation matures by facing reality. Its great shoulders of moral responsibility rise and begin to shake off its problems as a new resolve appears.

Perceptions of military and industrial threats from abroad are fueling the present concern over education, just as Sputnik did nearly 30 years ago. Then, private foundations (especially the Ford Foundation) and the government-sponsored National Science Foundation provided funds for curriculum reform. Although the dollar amounts of these grants appeared large in absolute terms, they were small in relation to the magnitude of the system ($100,000,000 is only $50 per classroom). Once developed, new curriculums had to be advertised, materials had to be disseminated, and teachers had to study new content and ways of teaching. As we will see, the overall impact of curriculum reform on the educational system was small.*

Our country does not have a central ministry of education than can be held accountable for the health of our schools. We have adopted a system of grass-roots governance in which 17,000 boards of education and their district administrations are responsible for the formulation of policy, and all citizens expect their views about educational policy to be taken seriously. However, neither school districts nor state departments of education are budgeted or staffed for expensive research and

---

*See: Goodlad and Klein (1970) and Goodlad (1983) for thoroughgoing descriptions of the impact (or more accurately, the lack of it) of the curriculum reform movement of the 1960s.

development activities, and even though federal and foundation funding has traditionally supported the development of new curriculums and teaching methods, local districts have had the option of using them or not. These innovations will simply languish, if local citizens and educators do not learn about them and put them to use.

Thus, in a real sense, everyone is responsible for the health of the schools. Blame for low quality or obsolescence cannot be deflected toward a central authority. If the schools are to be improved, we must all learn how to reflect on the alternative missions and means of schooling. We should all become "Monday-morning quarterbacks," each of us providing advice from our own perspective as a nonplaying coach. We also cannot pretend expertise we do not possess. All of us cannot master current educational technologies. We have to build, within the educational organization, a way that leading teachers and administrators can study the developing edge of research and learn to use it.

The problem of improving the schools — or even of deciding if they are as seriously troubled as their public image suggests — is unbelievably complex. We cannot simply tell a central ministry to get cracking and create good schools; we cannot hire an educational technologist to redesign the schools using the best existing knowledge; we cannot order 17,000 boards of education to drop everything and put all their energy into school improvement. We cannot even ask teachers to organize themselves to do the job, because we have confined their responsibilities to the classroom.

Although we have organized schools to deliver education, we have neglected to organize them so that planning school improvement is a normal part of the work of teachers and administrators — and that is what we must do now. We must learn to carry on what is esentially a national debate about the quality of education and how to improve it — but that debate must take place in thousands of local settings. We must learn to study what research and development experts can offer our schools. We must work with our political representatives to ease the grinding fiscal crises that have plagued education for so long. Most of all, we must regain our confidence that a union of education professionals and community members can be reforged to create the kind of education that all our children deserve and that current knowledge enables us to provide.

In the following pages the process of dialogue will receive the first attention as we examine complaints about the schools, our traditional ways of thinking about them, and ways we can come together productively. Then a series of recommendations will be made that capitalize on current knowledge about education and how to change it productively. Most interesting ideas about schooling die quickly for lack of nourishment in their action stages — we want to be in a position to create driving ideas that can shape the schools of the future and simultaneously create the conditions in which sensible ideas for school reform can thrive.

3

The Enigmatic Schoolhouse

The school floats paradoxically in an ocean of social forces. It is tightly clasped by tradition and yet is the medium of modern ideas and artifacts. It is the cradle of social stability and the harbinger of cultural change. Liberals and conservatives alike seek to make the school the instrument of social policy. Throughout history its critics have found it both too backward and too advanced. In simultaneous cadence it falls behind the times and fails to keep up with them.

As familiar as the school is, its missions are elusive. We have trouble arriving at a consensus. The inner city and the rural hinterland make their claims on creaky old schoolhouses while shiny suburban schools grope for a coherent mission. Basic education is prized but so are creativity, problem solving, academic excellence, and educational skills. The school's students are varied — talents and handicaps mingle, sometimes in the same minds and bodies. In the schools people with cultural differences are mixed together, and problems of identity and adaptation surface chaotically to be dealt with.

New technologies both strengthen the school's potential and threaten to replace it. School personnel receive very little training but are asked to manage one of the most complex professional tasks in our society. They have little status but awesome responsibility both for individual children and for the health of the society as a whole.

Because education exerts great influence on the young, society places great constraints on its schools, so that they will reflect prevailing social attitudes and current views about how children should be raised. The very size of the education system in this country draws attention. (In the United States there are more than 2 million education professionals, and about 8% of the gross national product is directly or indirectly consumed by the enterprises of education.) The public watches its investment carefully, scrutinizing educational practices, both traditional and innovative (Joyce & Morine, 1976).

Efficiency is highly prized, but innovations are watched with apprehension. Our societal patterns of schooling, established in the early 1800s, have become familiar and comfortable, and we want our children to have an education that has continuity with our own. Thus, most citizens are cautious about educational innovation. People praise the familiar old schoolhouse as much as they criticize it. They tend to believe that current problems in education are caused by changes (perceived as a "lowering of standards") — not by the reality that the old comfortable model of the school may be a little rusty and out-of-date. In fact, our society has changed a great deal since the days when the familiar and comfortable patterns of education were established, and many schools are now badly our of sync with the needs of children in today's world.

Schools, like all social institutions, tend to deteriorate unless they are continuously rejuvenated. When patterns of education become routine, life for the children and teachers in schools becomes less vital. The public faces a continuing dilemma: it must preserve familiar, traditional practices, making them as effective as possible, and yet keep up with the times in order to meet the challenges presented by social change. Thus, schooling exists in the middle of a social tug of war between proponents of tradition and proponents of change. As a result, much knowledge about what makes schools more effective is not being used.

The quality of education, as such, is not a controversial issue in our society. We may debate what kind of education is best for our children, but there is total agreement that schooling should be rigorous and effective. Even people who are not particularly dissatisfied with the current state of education usually believe that schooling can be improved. How to increase the effectiveness of schools is a more frustrating topic, and as people become more critical about the present state of schools, they become more frustrated.

4

Concerns and Accomplishments

We should not proceed much further without examining some of the most serious concerns that critics have voiced about our schools. We shall address these concerns in the form of replies to the questions that are most often raised.

Is the quality of our schools getting worse?

Because of the highly publicized decline in achievement-test scores, there is a general impression that the overall quality of our schools has declined, and that this decline cannot be totally accounted for by the expansion of the educational system to reach more and more students. In fact, there *has* been some decline in certain test scores, especially the test batteries most commonly given for college admission. However, these declines are not massive and do not occur in all areas. For example, reading achievement has dropped very little if at all. Many students cannot write well, but that was true in previous generations also.

However, there is reason to worry about achievement, because it has not *risen* dramatically over the last 30 years. With the aid of contemporary media, especially film, television, and the computer, our children should be vastly more literate than we were at their ages. Also, there has not been a rise in the proportion of students electing advanced science and mathematics courses, despite the attention given to scientific literacy. An easy comparison to make is that academic training has not kept pace with athletic training, where we have made great and visible strides over the last three decades. We need to ask, why not? And we need to do more.

Has the school as a melting pot failed and diluted its purpose?

Many people believe that the public school system is trying to do too much. It is being asked to cater to every conceivable kind of student with every conceivable kind of problem. This complaint suggests a surgical solution — that we should remove from our schools all those outside the mainstream — the slower learner, the disadvantaged, the foreign, and the handicapped, and let them make their own way, thereby creating schools that would serve only average and above-average students. In response to this complaint, we turn partly to evidence and partly to value positions.

First, studies of grouping practices consistently have indicated that students actually benefit from being in schools and classrooms that have a diversity of student abilities and backgrounds. With respect to academic learning, segregating usually hurts those with the lowest measures of academic ability — they learn less than when they are mixed with their more able peers — without helping those of greater ability. Also, social learning is enhanced when students mix with others who are different from themselves. Ability should not be regarded as fixed. In an educationally rich environment, some apparently unpromising students blossom. *Appropriate education raises intelligence.*

Second, if we are a society of variety, we must learn to work with variety. The gregarious, the shy, the lame, the sensitive, the timid, the whizzes, and the plodders must learn to share this planet for a lifetime. The bottom line: The more our schools assume responsibility for all our students the better off we will be.

Is the social climate out of control?

Almost every time an adult sees an insolent look on the face of an adolescent, that expression suggests a permissive, undemanding home and school environment. Low attendance is another visible symptom that something is wrong (large urban systems have absentee rates as high as 25%). Student abuse of elective-rich curriculums is still another signal that all is not well. One solution comes immediately to mind: tighten the standards, narrow the curriculum, and work the kids harder. In reality, however, a more vigorous social climate does not require narrowing of the curriculum. Effective schools reach students by teaching them how to learn in an increasing variety of ways.

Are the gifted and talented being neglected?

The specter of foreign competition and uncertainty in the job market prods us to worry about what we are doing with our most talented people. The notion has developed that our best and brightest spend their school years subjected to a slow-moving curriculum geared to the truant and the unmotivated. One solution is to create special schools to nurture talent. The problem is that talent comes in many forms and blossoms at different ages in different ways. To select visible talents early is to deny nourishment to latent talents. Our preferred solution is a more vigorous education for all!

Is the school out-of-date?

The dazzling advances we see in media and communications technology shock us, as we see at the same time rows of students taught by harried and unprepared teachers, and we realize that those students live in a world where intellectual communications sophistication are increasingly essential. The champions of the rich are concerned that the school environment is not rich enough to match the environment of the home. The champions of the poor are concerned that wealthier students' access *at home* to the computer and other contemporary technology will widen the gap between the advantaged and the poor. This prospect dismays the elitist and the egalitarian alike.

We believe that schools can be substantially improved through effective uses of technology. Electronic libraries do or should bring information to students in exponentially greater amounts. Films and television can bring the world's greatest teachers to all students. The best of art, music, science, and social science can be available to students in the most isolated schools if we will make it possible. Some changes are in order.

Have teachers gotten worse?

In the space of one short generation we changed from a society that was satisfied with teachers recruited from the upwardly mobile "lace curtain" poor and given one or two years of primitive normal school education, to one in which we wish teachers to both embody the renaissance of long ago and mingle its heritage productively with the technological sophistication of our society today. There is no evidence that teachers have gotten worse — in fact they are better educated than ever before. However, there is plenty of evidence that school curriculums haven't kept pace with the technological revolution. This is an educational lag that must be rectified. In reality, our investment in education is more at fault than our teachers, but teachers do need to go back to school on a regular basis — or they will fall behind. More about that later.

Will the negative publicity about education make it impossible to recruit good teachers in the future?

This is a difficult point. If schools are subjected to much more abrasive criticism from the press, recruitment may well become a problem.

Is teacher education in bad shape?

Almost everyone except teacher educators answer yes to this question, and many favor radical surgery to improve things. The most common complaint is that too much of the teacher preparation curriculum is devoted to "how to teach" and too little to "what to teach." In fact there is little basis for this particular concern because most teacher preparation is in the arts and sciences. Secondary teacher preparation curriculums require a major in the subject to be taught as well as a broad general education, and include very little instruction in curriculum and teaching methods. However, teacher education could be much more extensive and efficient than it is.

Are schools racist and establishmentarian?

Because schools must reflect society, our less-noble social views become incorporated into the structure of our educational institution. Schools simultaneously help rectify some inequalities while perpetuating others. On this issue we have real social tension.

Should we abandon our public school system in favor of private schools?

Critics increasingly express the belief that school decline will continue because the educational system is hopeless. One proposed solution is to redirect our resources into the private sector. Parents turn to private schools partly because they feel more powerful and effective in their dealings with them — if we don't like what a private school is doing we can move our sons and daughters to another one. Also, most private schools are small and social-class oriented. They do not have to deal with students whose parents cannot afford to pay. Schools select students (and parents select schools) on the basis of a shared conception of educational goals and strategies. Also, both schools and parents know that a private school can easily get rid of problem students who do not conform to its educational plan. The public school has no such option.

That individuals and organizations in our society should have the option to create schools and that citizens should have the right to choose them are not at issue. The issue is whether investment in public education should languish. There are two powerful arguments in favor of *increasing* investment in public education.

First, it manifests society's belief in the potential of all its people, regardless of their ability to pay or their special needs.

Public education is the cornerstone of social justice and fairness. Second, education is the bonding agent that welds us together despite our differences — our personal resources, talents, religions, races, languages, regions, and points of view. It provides a forum in which we learn about each other and how to work together to maximize our collective and individual potential.

Can the recent reports on education be believed?

Although the recent flood of highly publicized reports from foundations, government agencies, and professional organizations approach the problem of school improvement from somewhat differing frames of reference, the reports have surprising similarity in a number of areas.

All of the reports express overall concern with "excellence," which boils down to a desire to provide the young with a solid and vigorous education that will spawn habits of lifelong learning. Most of the reports suggest that schools can teach much more than they do, a point with which we agree, and that what they do teach can be taught better, another point that is hard to argue. Most emphasize that basic skills should be taught early and well and that the later education of students should be broad and powerful. Some reports emphasize early identification of the gifted and talented, some emphasize a Renaissance-style curriculum, some are concerned with restructuring the school.

John Goodlad (1983) would employ schools that are much smaller than those in many urban areas today. He would start schooling at age 4, in elementary schools with no more than 300 to 400 students, who eventually would pass on to high schools with no more than 600 to 800 students. He would have collegial teams of teachers — during the first years a student would stay with the same group of children and the same team of teachers in order to build a tightly knit learning community. Goodlad's report is unique in that it gives much more attention than do the others to the school improvement process. He believes that teachers should have 20 or more days a year to plan curriculum, to study academic content, and to develop their teaching skills.

Most of the reports recommend that we find ways to attract better teachers and give particular emphasis to science and mathematics. (The majority of the public is not aware that a serious shortage of mathematics and science teachers has existed for many years.) Some reports recommend merit pay as an incentive for excellence in teaching, and some suggest rewarding merit by providing the best teachers with time and money to help their peers.

On the whole, the reports assume, as we do, that we can vastly improve our schools. However, with the exception of Goodlad's report, they greatly underestimate what it takes to change a huge social institution, and they seriously neglect the investment in teaching personnel that must take place if schools are to change significantly. They also neglect the role of the public. Only a strong, unified public spirit will generate the deeds necessary to elevate our schools to the level that our children deserve.

ACCOMPLISHMENTS

Given the current welter of complaints about the educational system, it is easy to overlook its enormous accomplishment — what Lawrence Cremin (1965) calls the "genius of American education" — namely, the establishment of the common school in America. The magnitude of this accomplishment in the last 50 years alone is staggering. In 20 years, between 1940 and 1960, the size of the educational system virtually doubled; the workforce of teachers increased from about one to about two million, where it presently stands (see Joyce & Morine, 1976). During the same period we progressed from being a nation in which only 10% or 15% of the population received college education to one in which currently, in the more urbanized states, as many as 75% of high school graduates go on to receive some amount of higher education. More than 2 million teachers teach more than 40 million schoolchildren in 17,000 school districts in nearly 100,000 schools. Over 100,000 citizens are members of boards of education. In many states, public education is virtually free from preschool through the doctoral level, including advanced degrees in medicine, law, and the other professions.

We have accomplished this in a nation of remarkable diversity. Between 1945 and 1965 New York City absorbed a million immigrants from Puerto Rico alone. In Los Angeles, students identified as "minorities" now account for about 75% of the total school enrollment. (In California as a whole about 40% of students are so classified.) The enormous changes that have occurred in Eastern cities are reflected in the populations of their schools. Like the cities, the schools, too, have absorbed the impact of an enormous migratory trend. For example, the Washington, D.C., school district has been more than 90% black (both students and teachers) since around 1960, and because a large proportion of the black population of that city migrated from the South, many residents of the city are only first- or second-generation "Northerners." A similar picture exists throughout the large midwestern cities, Baltimore, Philadelphia, the northern New Jersey cities, and New York. Attempts to cope with legislated and de facto desegregation through busing and other programs have resulted in tremendously costly adjustments and in social disruption, all in the service of a good cause. The effort to provide additional services for students with learning difficulties has led to the creation of special programs for almost 16% of the nation's children, ranging from ones who are simply a bit slow in learning to those with truly serious physical, emotional, or mental handicaps. Over the last 10 years an enormous effort has been made to integrate these children into the "mainstream" of public education.

Unhappy citizens have been turning to the private sector in their serious search for a remedy that will cure the perceived ills of the public school system and better provide for the educational needs of their children. But before they abandon public education as a viable option, these people should pause and recall that this nation has a first-rate community college system, and that many of our great universities are public universities.

5

Some Popular Ideas
for Fixing the School

Given the complexity of the educational enterprise and the variety of points of view from which it is criticized, not to mention the general sense of frustration that results from feeling helpless in an unclear power situation, it would be surprising if all our thoughts about this complex situation were clear and rational. In fact, the dialogue about education commonly is sprinkled with several notions that are just enough awry to lead us down a primrose path of false expectations. We must learn to look out for the neat little traps these notions set for us. We need to exorcise some of these ideas before proceeding. Everyone will recognize them as familiar bromides.

Yesterday's good, solid schools provide the model for the future.

We are tempted to believe that schools will get better fast if we turn the clock back to the "good old days" and make education like it was when we were kids. This common notion ignores two important realities. The first is that today's commercial, industrial, and political leadership, which is losing its battles with foreign competition, was, in fact, educated in the "good old days." In fact, only in the last 30 years has our economic system faced the kind of competition it faces now. In a real sense we are being tested for the first time, and the result should be a clear warning that the way we were educated did not prepare many of us to manage ourselves in a way that stands up to genuine world-class competition. Conceivably, a return to the educational system of the past would simply exchange our current problems for the defects of a previous era, one whose schools were obsolete even in their time. The second reality is that schools have responded to the pressure to look backward for a model and probably have devoted more time to "basic skills" instruction — the staple of the "good old days" — during the last 15 years than at any time since the turn of the century. Over the last 15 years the amount of instructional time devoted to literature, writing, the arts, sciences, and social sciences has declined steadily as time spent on the bare-bones skills of reading and arithmetic has risen. It has been argued with some strength that the decline in national achievement-test scores can be attributed to the displacement of substantive education by the mechanics of reading and arithmetic. The decline certainly has been coincidental with the return to the "basics" that has been prompted by idealization of the "good old days."

Schools can be improved by insisting on higher standards.

Clearly, creating a consensus that schools need to be improved will be beneficial to public education. We need to debate the purposes of education and to select the most powerful means for achieving our objectives, and we need to develop assessment programs that realistically reflect these goals. However, we cannot simply set new goals and exhort the schools to achieve them. A massive social institution is very difficult to change. Yelling at it is relatively useless and fits into the same category of behavior as screaming at the post office to deliver the mail faster. Furthermore, we need to consider carefully who will set standards. If this responsibility is given to the national or state government the likely result will be greater standardization of education, and increased tensions between the opinions expressed at the national or state level and the traditional conduct of schooling at the local level. For example, in some states pressure to give more attention to the basic skills has resulted in the reduction of options for students to learn the sciences, social sciences, literature, and the arts. Thus, fewer educational opportunities exist now for students who have mastered the basic skills and for those who might best master them through the study of substantive subject matter. In California middle schools today, students receive four or five periods of physical education instruction from specialists each week, but they most likely receive no instruction at all in art, and in many cases their classes in science and social science are taught by nonspecialists. This situation is a result of a Byzantine tangle of regulations.

The point here is that the problems of the schools are too deep to solve by simply setting standards or piling on regulations and testing programs — which leads to a related idea that contains some neat traps and snares.

Schools can be improved without changing their operating structure.

The idea that cosmetic changes in the curriculum will result in significant educational improvement is seductive, but, in reality, the most important and difficult change that must be made is to prepare for the school improvement process. What is needed is a much larger investment in the school improvement process by teachers, administrators, and citizens. The amount of time given to planning and to re-educating the staff must be considerably increased. Currently, the investment of the education industry in staff development is far and away the lowest of any of our major institutions. The average teacher receives about 3 days of training each year, and in many districts only 1 or 2. School improvement, however, must become a regular part of the life of the organization: Teachers probably will need 20 or 30 days per year for renewal and for planning with other members of the faculty.

The structural problems of the school can be traced in part to the fact that for a century and a half the basic organizing unit of the school has been the classroom. It is so prominent a feature that most people have to search their memories to find examples of alternative forms of organization. Asked to build a school, most people — and most architects — would begin to arrange sets of boxes on paper until they had enough to accommodate the projected population of the school. Also, when we think of teachers, most of us think of *classroom teachers*. At the elementary level, we think of teachers who are in charge of almost the entire educational program for a group of students. At the upper levels, we think of teachers who are specialists in specific subjects. These teachers are assigned classrooms to which students come for instruction. Students migrate from classroom to classroom, receiving instruction from a variety of subject specialists.

Many alternatives to the organization of the school by classrooms have been proposed, and, in fact, much instruction takes place in such alternative structures, but the classroom has remained dominant to this day.

Two serious mistakes were made when the classroom structure was developed, mistakes that plague us today and have led to many of the problems that we now are trying to resolve. Both mistakes concern the job description of teachers. The first was that teachers were (and usually still are) expected to instruct during virtually the entire school day. Very little time was built into the job for preparation of lessons or for follow-up on the products of instruction (for example, for examining what students have written or the answers to problems they have tried to solve). Nor was time provided for teachers to study either academic content or the teaching process. Once trained, the teacher was (and is) assigned to a classroom, with the expectation that he or she would (and will) keep the students occupied essentially all day long, for the entire academic year. Even today, only four or five days a year are provided for in-service training or preparation. The second mistake was that no provision was made for teachers to get together and plan together — to think out the curriculum, select materials, discuss the progress of students, or coordinate their activities. Schools could have been organized so that staffs would arrive an hour or so before the students, to plan together without interruption or, just as easily, they could have been staffed in teams whose members would relieve one another, allowing each time for preparation and study. We can think of a lot of possibilities. However, the job specifications for the classroom teacher are like those for the least complex occupations in society — the jobs that can be done automatically without prior thinking or preparation and without coordination. The effects of working under these conditions are considerable, and can be seen in the organizational behavior of teachers and administrators, in the attitudes of the community toward teaching, and in the problems attendant to school improvement efforts.

First, most schools are, in reality, a set of individual miniature schools called classrooms. Teachers learn to be responsible for discipline within their territory, to scan their students for signs of ill health, to create a miniature social system within which they can carry out instruction. They work in unbelievable isolation from their colleagues, tied down as they are within their cells. They become self-reliant and more than a bit cynical about their leaders, with whom they have relatively little contact when they are working.

The community has come to expect that teachers will do their jobs without having time for preparation or renewal, and it sees the curriculum as what the teacher does, not as what the faculty has constructed. In many communities there is resistance to providing time to teachers for renewal or for cooperative planning. Time for in-service work or curriculum development is regarded as time taken from the job, rather than as something that adds to teachers' effectiveness.

The situation teachers are in is analogous to a manufacturing firm whose workers have no time to develop new products and whose salespersons must operate without meetings to discuss products or sales strategies. Thus, the entire process of school improvement becomes very difficult. The absence of time for teachers to collectively plan or to individually study academic subjects, instructional materials, and the process of teaching, makes it extremely difficult for the faculty either to invent improvements or to tool themselves up to utilize ones from outside the school. As mentioned earlier, the level of implementation of the powerful new curriculums that are available in academic areas has been very low. Time has not been provided for learning to use media and educational technology, and therefore these teaching aids do not easily find a way into the program of the school. Further, because classroom teachers are isolated, they rarely watch one another at work, and thus have very little opportunity to borrow ideas from their colleagues.

The finger of blame can be easily and accurately pointed.

As stated earlier, the educational system is massive, but at the same time it is locally controlled and is intertwined with the entire society. Thus, the children of the society bring to school the problems as well as the virtues with which we have imbued them. Over 2 million American citizens are teachers and more than 40 million children attend our schools. These children are the offspring of about 40 million parents. About 100,000 citizens sit on the boards of governance of the nation's 17,000 school systems. Despite periodic alarm that the federal and state governments have achieved too much control, governance rests firmly in the hands of local boards of education and professional educators, and the day-to-day education of our nation's children is governed by the 2 million teachers who work essentially in autonomy and with pathetically little support or supervision from the tiny staffs of curriculum specialists who have survived the budget cuts made in the years of fiscal austerity. Federal and state roles usually are confined to providing minimal financial support and to attempting to maintain minimal standards for quality in certain areas of the operation. With such a huge system and with so many citizens involved, the schools clearly are a part of all of us. If blame should be assigned, then we all have to share it. It is ironic that so many members of the public feel ineffective to improve education when so many of us are involved and in fact do control the system.

How common is finger-pointing in debates over the improvement of education? All too common, unfortunately.

We can see it quite clearly as boards of education have become more politicized — in many cases board membership has become a political stepping-stone — and board elections have become an arena for reassessing the adequacy of school administrations. The longevity of superintendents has decreased, so that the average superintendent now stays a little less than three years in one position! Not infrequently the reason superintendents leave their position is connected to a change in the composition of the school board. The scenario goes like this:

> The board election is surrounded by debate about the adequacy of the schools. The majority of the newly elected board members played no role in selecting the resident superintendent. The new board wishes to wield a new broom — and either makes life so uncomfortable for the incumbent superintendent that he leaves voluntarily, or they buy up his contract and fire him outright. They conduct a search for a new superintendent and find one, heralding him as the leader the schools have always needed. About the time he is adjusted to his new duties, there is another election. The election is conducted amidst a debate about the quality of the schools. The new board . . .

The effect is to greatly decrease the efficiency of the school administration by lowering commitment to long-term planning. As long as this scenario persists, both new boards and new superintendents have a stake in repudiating or ignoring long-term school improvement efforts generated by their predecessors. This has a demoralizing effect on the middle-management administrators who gear up to improve a curriculum area or to increase the use of an educational technology only to find that the priorities have changed and they now must abandon that effort —they watch the investment that has already been made get thrown to the winds and now gear up for something else that may be abandoned as the political winds change.

Teachers, of course, see all this as a game played by boards and administrators who live in a reality that is completely different from their own. They learn that initiatives come and go, but children continue to enroll in schools that have ever-decreasing resources, while people far removed from teachers — their leadership — act as if they were in charge and posture for the press.

Another effect of this scenerio is to draw school boards and central administrations toward short-term initiatives that can be dramatized in the press. We see this at the state level: headlines announce "Literacy tests to be given to all teachers" (as if to say our teachers are generally illiterate!). We see it at the district level: "Tougher graduation standards initiated" (implying that whatever is wrong with 12 years of education will be corrected by denying graduation to a few of the children of the poor!). We see it in reports that purport to speak to the national condition of education: "Recommend adding 5 days to school year." All of these remedies are designed to attract attention, can be implemented quickly, and involve minimal or no dollar cost; these kinds of exhortations and attempts to set standards put pressure on teachers and students without investing in the process of school improvement. Changing a school, however, is quite difficult and requires great determination and long-term efforts — a subject we will return to later.

What is ironic about the political dynamics now so typical of board - superintendent relations, about the growing emphasis on initiatives that stress dramatic, cosmetic, short-run, bottom-line results, is that they create the same conditions that have caused the decline of so many American businesses, especially the ones that must contend with foreign competition. This short-run view, this tendency to please the board with spurious single-year results, when it is clear that the long run is what matters, has made our economic investment policies extremely vulnerable to patient planners with long-term orientations. This same viewpoint, applied to education, socializes the public to think there are quick fixes for whatever ails education, but just as there are no quick fixes for the economy, there are none for our educational system, an institution that involves virtually the entire population.

The citizens who campaign to be elected to boards of education should not be blamed for this condition, but it is also clear that they are liable to be unwitting accomplices in a process that weakens executive authority in the system, alienates teachers from them and from their professional leadership, and creates conditions wherein a large proportion of the energy of the executives is occupied in dealing with conflict among the members of the boards of governors.

The innovations of the sixties and seventies made the schools worse.

Derived partly from the urge to return the schools to the familiar forms we knew as children and partly from the search for something to blame for our discontents, there is a tendency to believe that the problems in our educational system were caused, at least in part, by curriculum innovations that were initiated in the last quarter-century. The New Mathematics, the New Science, and other academically oriented reforms within the curriculum areas are sometimes blamed for the decline in "basic skills" achievements. Nothing could be further from the truth, and there is hard evidence on this point.* When academic reforms in specific subjects were implemented, student achievement rose in those subjects and in related skill areas as well. Some of these programs even managed to raise the aptitude of students and, in a few cases, intelligence test scores rose. But there is a deep suspicion of educational innovation and it creates a tendency to blame innovative curriculums for current problems. Hence, some innovations have been rejected even though they clearly benefited the children in the schools that used them. Ironically, those reforms generated a very important kind of educational research dealing with the dynamics of education. Investigators have learned that the innovations were used in relatively few schools, that those schools made a much greater investment in in-service teacher education than is the norm, and that the administrators of the districts made a much greater effort to assist in the innovative process than is usual in most school districts. We learned from the innovative period that curriculum change requires much more dedication and redirection of resources than was previously thought to be the case (Fullan, 1983).

Most schools did not implement curriculum innovations to a degree sufficient to affect achievement either upwardly or downwardly.

Severe criticism of many other innovations that proved successful when well implemented has occurred even though they led to a better quality of education. Bilingual and multicultural programs to equalize educational opportunity, such as Head Start and Follow-Through, certainly did not hurt achievement and in many cases had beneficial results. Like the innovations in curriculum, for example, the New Mathematics and the New

---

*For a summary, see: Joyce, Showers, Dalton, and Beaton (1985).

Science, these socially oriented programs also were difficult to implement, but where they have been implemented they have done well.

Getting rid of the poor students will do the trick.

Education has been a mainstay of the American Dream — it is thought to provide the key to upward mobility and to social unity. Yet, as the proportion of people who attend school grows larger and more diverse, schools must adapt more to meet the needs of individuals and groups who have trouble succeeding in the school milieu. In many inner-city schools, attendance figures are as low as 50% to 75%. Recent immigrants try to learn in settings where their language is not spoken. Students such as these struggle with assignments that their college-bound classmates breeze through.

It is tempting to take a survival-of-the-fittest orientation. One of the recent national school-reform reports suggests lowering the age at which students can leave school and confining our investment to children who are well adapted to the school as it is.

The assumption of this proposal is that schools will be able to do a better job with the more able if they get rid of the less able. But this assumption does not stand up to the evidence. It has not been proved that segregating the more talented is beneficial to them, but it definitely hurts those who are less able. Some schools and school districts do very well with a wide variety of children. (The schools that don't might pay greater attention to the ones that succeed.) Also, some well-researched and successful programs are not widely used, even though these programs go a long way toward solving the problem of educating students of diverse talents; in fact, these programs have demonstrated not only their effectiveness in reaching the less talented, or the less motivated, but also their potential to increase academic aptitude and motivation.*

We will pay an enormous future social cost if we ignore children who do not immediately respond to the average school

*See: Slavin, 1982; Spaulding, 1970.

environment. We have an obligation to use the procedures that work, rather than saying we will not change the schools, and will leave the children we neglect to take the future consequences.

Proposals to neglect students who do not fit in, because doing so will benefit the remainder, are wrong — both because the expected benefits will not ensue and because there are viable alternatives. On a humane level, all children deserve the best we can give them to help them achieve the highest quality of life. On a social level, the future of our society depends on a fully educated society in which each person contributes to their potential. To despair of creating schools where all children can learn productively is to deny our creativity and the reality that all students are benefited by the mixture of talents, emotions, needs, and perspectives that are contributed to the community of the school.

There is little research about how to improve education —our opinions are probably as good as the implications of the knowledge base.

So much negative publicity has been directed at education professors and innovative programs that it is not surprising that much of the public — and even many education professionals —is unaware of the growing base of knowledge about how to approach many of the important problems of schooling and teaching.

Several thousand educational researchers have been trained in the last 25 years and, even though the public investment in educational research has been pitifully small (and is declining), that cadre is very active in accumulating knowledge at a steady rate. If funding for educational research is not totally decimated, that knowledge will now begin to increase exponentially.

There is already a fairly solid knowledge base about many important issues. Just as important, knowledge about how to bring about sensible improvements in education has increased dramatically. We know something about the most effective schools and teachers, about productive leadership, about how to implement more powerful curriculums, about how to use technology to benefit students, and we have quite a storehouse of effective teaching methods and curriculums.

What we need to do is to learn how to use that knowledge. This requires, first, that people believe it exists. Many boards and central administrations discuss, without reference to the existing knowledge base, how to group children, how to reach the "slower" or "less-motivated" students, what curriculums to choose, and how to invest in technology; they seem to believe they can operate de novo.

During a consultation with a school district, I attended a board of education meeting and heard one board member state that the use of microprocessors in schools would lead to a generation of "arcade junkies." He even suggested that his assertion was based on research. No other member of the board of central administration of that district of more than 100 schools could refute him, except by voicing another equally unproven opinion, although he was talking through his hat. Confronted with the fact that I did have some evidence and was regarded as an authority on educational research, he proceeded to try to discredit the educational research community as a band of axe-grinders. Fortunately, he overplayed his hand and undermined his position by his outrageous use of hyperbole, so the children in that community will not be denied the tools of the times. Although extreme, this board member is not so different from, for example, those who debate whether or not to group children by ability, and do so without reference to the substantial knowledge base that exists on the costs and benefits of that practice, or those who think that lengthening the school day or year without making qualitative changes, will do the trick.

SUMMARY

As the next chapter will show, we have a fairly good knowledge base on which we can build a gradual but solid program of reform that eventually will produce dramatic results. And, if we have the will and work together, we can get some real results quite quickly.

II

VISIONS OF
EFFECTIVE SCHOOLING

6

Scenes from a School

Children who are entering school today can expect to be alive in 2060. The technological developments that so dazzle today's world will have been replaced by then by others that are only dimly conceived today. National and world societies also will change substantially: great nations are rising and the planet is becoming fully populated; colonies may well be established on other planets; life in cities will change even more radically than in the past; in melting-pot societies like the United States, races and ethnic groups will have to come to new accommodations and people will live on more productive terms. We attempt here to build a model school that can prepare students to grow throughout their lives. We want to build a school that will prepare students to absorb and to make productive the technological and social changes that lie before them. The solutions of today will have to give way to the solutions of tomorrow if we want to retain our fundamental values about the quality of life and human dignity. As we try to rethink the school we draw on a rich heritage of many models of education that have been developed by both visionaries and practical inventors.

Within each of the curriculum areas (reading, arithmetic, social studies, science, the performing arts, physical education, etc.), research and development efforts have generated a vast number of alternative approaches. Educational technologists have labored to generate new ways of using media and new approaches to the organization of schools. Architects have developed ways of matching physical plants to educational models and of developing facilities that are adaptable to a wide variety of ends and means.

In the pages that follow, we will visit a teaching team in the Jefferson Elementary School. Our purpose is to look at a very modern school that incorporates many recent developments in staffing arrangements and technology. Also, because Jefferson presents a number of ways of teaching, it permits us to explore a variety of forms of effective schooling.*

THE DIRECT-INSTRUCTION TEAM

Harvey is the team leader of an elementary school direct-instruction team that consists of eight members including an assistant to the team leader, named Marge (see Table 6.1). Harvey and Marge are jointly responsible for the direction of the team and the continuing education of its members. He is a science specialist and she is a reading specialist. In every elementary school direct-instruction team, one of the two leadership positions is filled by a reading specialist, because the team does a great deal of reading instruction, although it is not the only provider of reading instruction. Harvey and Marge are responsible for creating and carrying out the operating curriculums for 200 children. These curriculums are tailored to the special characteristics of the children, the school community, and the subject matter. They are guided by curriculum plans created by the area curriculum council, which is composed of curriculum specialists from all subject areas plus representatives from each direct instruction team.

---

*All of the elements of the Jefferson school are drawn from existing schools I have visited. In fact, except for the microprocessor, I saw each of the elements more than 20 years ago, when I wrote an article that eventually became the first draft of this description. The technologies are described more fully in Joyce, Hersh, and McKibbin (1983).

TABLE 6.1. THE DIRECT-INSTRUCTION TEAM

	TEACHER LEADERS		
Harvey			Marge
	TEACHERS		
George			Florence
	PARAPROFESSIONALS		
Joan	Maureen	Tommy	Mary

Two other members of the team have professional status. One is George, a young teacher with a strong background in the social sciences, who hopes to become a specialist in computer-assisted instruction. Harvey and Marge arrange for him to work as much as possible with the computer support center. The other, Florence, a middle-aged woman who is returning to teaching after an absence of several years, expects to become a reading specialist, and much of her in-service training therefore is Marge's responsibility. The four other membrs of the team are para-professionals. Two, Joan and Maureen, are college graduates; one has a degree in the social sciences and the other has her degree in mathematics. Both have completed a special course to prepare them to work with a direct-instruction team, and expect to continue their professional preparation and to become certified teachers. As part of this preparation they are assigned for one year to a direct-instruction team. The following year they will be rotated among the instructional support centers for further in-service preparation. Tommy, one of the paraprofessionals, is a high school graduate, 19 years old, who is unsure about his future. He and many other youngsters like him are attached to direct-instruction teams and instructional support centers throughout the district, where they work under close supervision. At the end of each year, Tommy and his peers discuss with the personnel director their future roles and educational plans. As long as they remain attached to instruction teams, they are required to be enrolled in programs to further their education. Mary, the fourth paraprofessional, is also a high school graduate. She is married and the mother of two, and is a warm, supportive person who tends to gather around her the shy and lonely children. She takes responsibility among other things, for the orientation of the children who are new members of the direct-instruction team.

In one sense, about 25 parents also are members of the team. Several serve as part-time volunteer (unpaid) aides to the team, and Harvey and Marge operate a regular parent-tutoring series in which they explain the children's educational program and inform parents about ways of helping the children at home.

Harvey and his assistant deploy the direct-instruction team as required by their plans. Although certain kinds of teaching are done only by the professionals within the team or the instructional support centers, all team members, including the paraprofessionals, function in teaching roles. The paraprofessionals, more often than the professionals, set up equipment, maintain the environment as an attractive and efficient place, and help the children move from place to place. As they gain experience and confidence, the paraprofessionals are able to engage in more significant teaching.

SUPPORT CENTERS

Harvey's staff also includes professionals and paraprofessionals from six instructional support centers. Together with parent volunteers they form Harvey and Marge's extended staff. The staffs of each of these centers are specialists who create or organize instructional materials and programs and are available as consultants to members of the direct-instruction teams. Let us look at the instructional support centers (see Figure 6.1 and Table 6.2).

Computer Support Center

In this center are specialists who apply computer technology to curriculum and instruction problems. They develop and adapt computer simulations, and automate programmed instructional materials created by others and used in the self-instruction center. They work with the diagnostic and counseling centers to automate diagnostic procedures and to help the direct-instruction team

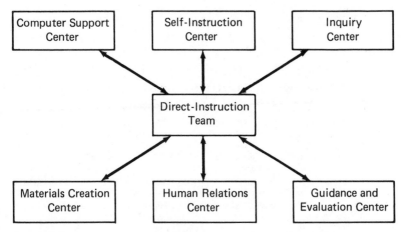

FIGURE 6.1   Direct-Instruction Teams and Support Centers

automate the scoring of objective tests in order to track the progress of the children. One computer support center serves about 20 direct-instruction teams. For many applications, it uses a large computer which, in turn, is used by many other support centers scattered throughout the region. The Jefferson center includes two teachers who are specialists in computer-assisted instruction, several paraprofessionals, some of whom are computer programmers, and temporary personnel who are attached to the center for various purposes.

Self-Instruction Center

This center, which serves five or six direct-instruction teams, provides programmed materials and many self-instruction packets prepared by the staff in consultation with subject specialists and members of the direct-instruction teams. It uses computer-based instruction for many purposes, including self-instruction programs in mathematics and science purchased from commercial firms. The staff is available to develop specialized materials for those direct-instruction teams for which it is responsible. For example, the staff has developed packets of readings in various subject areas that are used in the nearby high school. The self-instruction center library is available for use by the direct-instruction team. This library has access to electronic information systems and to videotape and film services. Sometimes children are taken there for extra work or special assignments and its staff helps monitor their progress. What is important about self-instruction centers is that they have the capacity not only to adapt materials created by commercial firms and research agencies, but also to develop materials that serve the particular needs of the direct-instruction team.

TABLE 6.2. INSTRUCTIONAL SUPPORT CENTERS

	Function	*Staff*	*Serves*
Materials Creation	Create visual/written materials Work with DIT* Develop material for inquiry Assist self-instruction center specialists Film preparation (e.g., current events newscast)	2 media specialists 6 professional writers, artists, musicians (part-time)	20 DITs** 3 self-instruc-tion centers
Inquiry	Library/media center with books, tapes, records, film strips, slides Data storage and retrieval terminals Consult with DIT on resource units Large-group instruction assistance Assist in staff development Professional library	2 librarian/media specialists 2 specialists in humanities and sciences 6 paraprofessionals	6-7 DITs
Self-instruction	Prepare self-instruction units in math, science, social studies, spelling, grammar, and high school science, mathematics and social studies Assist DIT in unit development and presentation	6 specialists in math, science, social science, art, music, children's literature 6 paraprofessionals 20 volunteers	5-6 DITs Elementary and high school specialists help in inquiry

TABLE 6.2. INSTRUCTIONAL SUPPORT CENTERS *continued*

	Function	*Staff*	*Serves*
Human Relations	Counseling Human relations training Diagnostic problems in DIT social systems Small-group organization Create staff development programs Organizational development Quality Circles Problem solving	6 counselors 2 paraprofessionals	10 DITs
Guidance and Evaluation	Diagnosis/prescription Create special tests and assessment devices Career charting (teachers, aides, interns)	4 counselor/ evaluators 2 psychometrists 1 statistician	5-6 DITs
Computer Support	Computer simulation Programmed instruction Diagnostic development, testing, automation Support for all other centers	2 CAI specialists 2 programmers 2 paraprofessionals	20 DITs 5 inquiry centers 5 self-instruction centers 10 guidance centers 20 materials creation centers

*DIT = Direct-Instruction Team
** 1 DIT = 20 students

Human Relations Center

The human relations center is staffed by professionals and paraprofessionals who provide counseling and human relations training to students and staff. For example, a direct-instruction team might call on the human relations center to help diagnose and correct a cooperative learning problem within a student group. A human relations expert then might be dispatched to work with a small group of children, helping them to organize and work together more efficiently. Other children might be sent to the human relations center for a special program designed to increase their capacity for and flexibility in interpersonal relations. The human relations center, however, is not a "life adjustment" factory, devoted to subordinating individuals to the interests of the group. On the contrary, its purpose is to help resolve problems in human relations so that both group and individual learning needs are satisfied.

Inquiry Center

The inquiry center is a library in the most advanced sense of the word. It provides films, tape recordings, and other materials children can use as they carry out personal inquiries. Facilities are provided for listening to tapes and records, for viewing motion pictures, film strips, and slide collections, and for retrieving electronically stored data. Professionals and paraprofessionals on the inquiry center staff help children use the facilities, help shape students' inquiries, and are responsible for stocking adequate materials in each subject area. The staff also consults with members of the direct-instruction teams on the development of instructional units. Sometimes inquiry center staff members participate as teachers. They give lectures and demonstrations to large groups, and work with the team leaders to conduct in-service training programs for team members.

Materials Creation Center

The staff of the materials creation center consists of professional writers, artists, and audiovisual specialists who are responsible for creating visual and written materials tailored to the learning needs of the students in the area. They work with the staffs of both the direct-instruction teams and the independent inquiry centers. For example, a direct-instruction team together with the social studies specialist may desire to create materials for a unit on one of the new nations of the world. They consult with the staff of the materials creation center to produce readable new materials for all the children, including those with special needs.

The materials creation center might develop projects on its own, but its primary purpose is to serve the needs of the direct-instruction teams and the specialists in the independent inquiry centers, thus freeing the school from dependence on commercial firms whose materials cannot be specifically keyed to local needs and interests.

Guidance and Evaluation Center

This center works with both the computer support staff and the human relations staff to help the direct-instruction team diagnose and make prescriptions for individual progress. It creates special tests and other assessment devices. Staff counselors work with children to identify intellectual growth and to make prescriptions pertaining thereto. The guidance and evaluation staff does the test making for most direct-instruction teams, although some teams prefer to make their own and rely on the center primarily for advice and technical assistance.

A DAY WITH A DIRECT-INSTRUCTION TEAM TEACHER

8 A.M., October 22: Harvey convenes the meeting of his direct-instruction staff to discuss two educational programs. One project involves the computer support center, whose technicians have developed a model that simulates the economic activities of a store. Harvey, his staff, and the computer staff are all engaged in creating a simulation that will teach students the economic principles that operate as a store purchases goods, sets prices, creates advertising programs, and organizes its personnel. The students will learn these principles by making decisions in a game-type situation. For example, as they make decisions about the price of a product, they will receive feedback on sales and will be able to adjust prices, advertising, and other factors to see if they can increase the product's profit. Although the program has been used successfully with older children, this is the first attempt within this school district to apply the technique to the 7 - 9 age bracket. Thus, one member of the guidance and evaluation center is observing the process and offering advice about the testing program. The social-science specialist from the independent inquiry center also is present, as an observer and consultant, because if the experiment works there may be uses for the material in that center. During the meeting, Harvey and his staff select 20 children for their trial run. If all goes well, the number of students who participate gradually will be increased. Although the direct-instruction team has much help from the computer center personnel, Harvey wants to proceed slowly so that the members of his own team can train themselves to use the simulation effectively and to follow it up with additional instruction outside the computer support center. He also wants to give George some practice and a chance to explore further his interest in becoming a specialist in computer applications.

The other project the direct-instruction team discusses is their fine arts program. Using visitors, the local art museum, and specialists from the creative arts and humanities staffs of the high school, they have developed a unit on Renaissance art for use in the social studies program. Some staff members have reported a total lack of interest in Renaissance art among the students. They arrange for one of the museum specialists, who believes she is having great success with the children, to hold a demonstration later that day, so the staff can observe how she treats the content. Some of the team are dubious about the value of the unit in general. Mary is assigned to discuss with the children their reactions to the program.

The meeting ends at 8:40 A.M. and Harvey goes over his notes for a science seminar. Marge gathers Maureen, Tommy, and Joan, and until 9 A.M. they discuss some of the problems they are having in the reading program.

9:00 A.M.: Harvey leads 10 children in a discussion of a science project. This group has built a static electricity generator and is conducting a set of experiments with it. Science is Harvey's own subject specialty; he regularly handles two science project groups — an advanced group (this one) and a group of rather difficult children whom he hopes to reach through their interest in science. Tommy observes Harvey during the discussion, because he will be following up on what Harvey does during the rest of the week.

While Harvey's discussion goes on, the rest of the team is deployed variously. Mary and Maureen lead a number of children to the independent inquiry center, where they help them select books. Joan and Laura accompany another group of children to the self-instruction center, where the children work on self-instruction materials to develop reading skills. This program was set up by Marge, in consultation with the self-instruction support center. It is Joan and Laura's job to administer the program and to give personal help to the students as needed. At the same time, Marge is working with a group of slow readers who have not been responding to self-instruction materials. She has developed an experience approach for them that tailors their activities to their specific needs.

George watches as the computer center technicians prepare the simulated store. Before the hour is over, Tommy leaves Harvey's discussion and sets up a large-group instruction room for a current events film that will be shown during the next hour to many of the children. This film has been created by the materials creation center, in response to requests from several teams who felt that not enough materials were available for teaching current events to 7- to 9-year-old children. They were concerned that many children in that age group do not benefit either from commercial television newscasts or from the weekly films prepared by local news agencies. Consequently, during this year the materials creation specialists are filming a short newscast each week and distributing it to the various direct-instruction teams.

10:00 A.M.: Harvey and George are in the computer support center watching their students operate the simulated store. The operation goes well. The children are able to cope with the problems they are given and are excited about their work. The experience is so positive that the decision is made to continue the program with that group on a regular basis and then to expand its use to another group. Harvey makes arrangements to brief the computer staff on the social studies program on which the simulation is based. Harvey and George discuss ways of establishing relationships between the store game and the rest of the program. It is George's task to see that follow-up takes place when the children return to their direct-instruction team.

Harvey also makes arrangements for two members of the computer support staff to bring the simulated store directly into the team suite after the trial period is over. He thinks the trials should be held in the computer support center area, where he and the computer support staff can review and revise the materials, until it is time to integrate them into the social studies program.

Also, while he is there, Harvey discusses with the center's director some new spelling programs that the director says have just come on the market. Harvey's students have been doing very well with these programs, and the director has informed him that if computer assistance is added to them, the programs could be used with teams throughout the school district. However, until computer assistance is obtained, use of the programs is restricted to Harvey's team and perhaps one other, because evaluation of student progress is so laborious.

10:50 A.M.: Harvey watches the end of the discussions of the current events film being conducted by Laura, Marge, Joan, and Maureen. Joan has made a tape recording of the session so that Harvey or Marge can help her analyze and improve her teaching. It is a matter of team routine that each week members tape or videotape a lesson and then review it with another team member. Also, the team routinely makes videotape recordings of large-group presentations and then determines whether to place them in the file at the inquiry center for later use. The value of videotaping lectures or demonstrations is that the original presentation can then be used with different groups in a variety of ways.

11:00 A.M.: Harvey spends most of the hour preparing a set of creative writing activities that will be used with most of the children in the instruction group. He and the team have decided that too little spontaneous writing has been coming from the group, so they intend to try a set of stimulator activities to involve the children in creative writing. Harvey designs the activities so that all 200 children will be grouped into teams that will write collections of poems, stories, plays, radio dramas, and a newspaper. Staff members of the team will act as consultants for the various groups. The work of each student team will be used to stimulate the members of the other teams.

While Harvey prepares this unit, Marge and Maureen work with a small group of children making a videotape that will be used in the arithmetic program. Other staff members of the direct-instruction team have taken children to the self-instruction center to work on arithmetic programs, and to the independent inquiry center to work on projects in the social studies. Four children have gone with Tommy to the human relations center, where they have a session one day each week with one of the counselors.

12:00 noon: Harvey eats lunch with Mary and a small group of children. He and Marge each have lunch with a different group of children each day, so that every other week every child has an intimate and informal half hour with one of the two team leaders. Mary accompanies Harvey because these children have recently transferred to the team from another school district. Her job is to make them comfortable and welcome, to get to know them, and to transmit any important personal information to Harvey and Marge. One of the girls having lunch with Harvey was in the group that operated the simulated store that morning, and Harvey persuades her to describe to the others what she did and to tell them how she felt about it. This, of course, provides him with a child's-eye view of the simulation activity. As he listens he notes that she has not yet connected the work of the store with the rest of the social studies program. After only one experience with the store, it is natural that the gadgetry and its operation will fill her mind, but he thinks to himself that he must be careful to keep track of the students' perceptions of what they are learning.

1:00 P.M.: Almost all the children are engaged in small-group or individual activities. Many of them are in the self-instruction center; some are in the independent inquiry center. Marge and Laura each have a small remedial reading group gathered around them. Harvey and Tommy take this morning's science group to the independent inquiry center so the children can hunt for materials for their next set of science experiments. When he is satisfied that Tommy can handle the situation, Harvey returns to the team suite and prepares the large-group instruction area, where a member of the art staff will work during the next hour. He explains to the art consultant that the team has been having great difficulty with the Renaissance art unit. The consultant agrees to make a demonstration tape of his discussion with a small group of children for the staff to examine. Also, because some of the staff's problems may be caused by their own inadequate knowledge of art, the consultant calls his office and arranges for another art specialist to observe during the small-group discussion period, to get some idea as to whether the problem is with the teachers or with the choice of subject matter.

2:00 P.M.: Harvey listens to the art lecture and prepares to follow up with his small group. At the beginning of this unit, videotapes were used for the large-group meetings, but the children did not respond actively to them, so the instruction team decided to use live speakers for short periods of time, followed by discussions, some to be conducted by the art consultants. Today, the art consultant has brought along a suit of armor and a set of weapons from the medieval period. Many of the boys in the group are enthusiastic. As Harvey observes the children's reactions he wonders whether it might not be best to concentrate more on the social life of the times, integrating art units like this one with social studies units, rather than treating the art by itself, as they have attempted to do in this unit.

In the conference afterwards Harvey and the art consultant discover that they have simultaneously come to the same conclusion —the Renaissance art unit is going extremely well with the older, more verbal students and not at all well with the others. With Marge, they come to a rapid decision to continue the program for one or two more days, and then, if their feelings are confirmed, to extend the unit with the students for whom it seems to be productive and to create a completely different type of activity for the other students.

3:00 P.M.: For 20 minutes, half the team listens to and criticizes tapes or videotapes of lessons conducted by the other half of the team. Harvey plays a tape of his morning science discussion, and Marge critiques it for him. They both notice that one child has contributed very heavily to the discussion session. Marge also questions whether the hypotheses the group set up were as well worded and explicit as they might have been. Harvey feels that these criticisms are accurate. They next discuss ways they can help to sharpen students' thinking.

3:30 P.M.: Over coffee, Marge conducts a meeting with the entire staff about the reading program. She has some suggestions for individual conferences, and presents a report from the self-instruction center about the students' progress with word-attack skills. The team's objective is to get the children to teach themselves everything possible, which would free their instruction time with teachers for learning things they have difficulty teaching themselves. Marge has set up the reading program so that almost all of it consists of individual conferences during which the children discuss their progress in using self-instruction materials and identify projects and reading for independent inquiry. Small groups are formed for remedial work and for the children who do not seem to work well by themselves. Mary's role is to work with the children who have trouble keeping themselves focused on individual learning tasks. Her tactics are motherly and supportive, whereas Marge is rather brisk and direct, so they arrange to work with the children for whom their styles are most effective.

4:00 P.M.: All the team members are working independently, preparing for the next day. Harvey prepares the agenda for tomorrow's meeting, at which he will explain the creative writing unit and the staff will discuss it. He also prepares a mathematics lesson for one group of older children. Marge finishes some correspondence for the team (they share a secretary with another team). George spends the hour with the computer support center planning the next day's use of the simulated store. Laura matches self-instruction reading units to students' needs over the next few days. Each day she does this for a certain number of children, thus each child's progress is reviewed either by her or by Marge at least once every two weeks. Joan, Maureen, and Tommy are in the independent inquiry center, developing resource units to be used with the next set of social studies programs.

The Team and the Teacher

Harvey is a teacher with a large and complex staff who can do many things. He is not simply a master teacher — one who works better with children than anyone else or who knows his subject better than anyone else. Harvey also is a master at coordinating the work of other people and at developing curriculum patterns that are tailored to the individual needs of the children in his group, to the community in which they live, to the requirements of the subject matter, and to the large variety of instructional materials at hand. His staff includes the seven members of his direct-instruction team plus the specialists within the various support centers. Harvey and his staff provide an individualized education that blends attention to each child's interests, needs, and personal problems with the best educational technologies available. The direct-instruction team members are the final decision makers in the educational process; therefore, judgments about what each child will do and learn are made by the people who know him or her the best.

KINDS OF LEARNING

Harvey and his team orchestrate an environment that reaches the children in three ways: (1) *personal inquiry* (students pursue an interest of their own); (2) *independent study* (students work with materials geared to their ability levels and, through the use of these materials, learn to teach themselves); and (3) *group inquiry* (students inquire into problems that are important to them and appear significant to their teachers). Let us look more closely at these three kinds of learning.

Personal Inquiry

Harvey and his staff help the children arrange their time so that a good proportion of each week is spent pursuing projects the children select and carry out alone or in small groups, with help provided, as needed, by the teachers. For example, the students select books to read for pleasure but consult with the teachers about these. The teachers try to persuade each student to write or record something of personal significance every week, whether it be a story, essay, something dictated into a tape recorder, or something written for production by a group. The children pursue topics that interest them: one month they may study snails in great depth; another month they may read the poems of Robert Frost; yet another month they may study the history of baseball. Several times each week each student meets with one teacher to discuss his or her personal inquiry program and the resources needed to carry it out. If a student needs a book or a telescope, for example, these can be found in the independent inquiry center. If someone is having trouble finding clay for a sculpture, the teacher will help that student find it. Harvey's direct-instruction team makes sure that each child has a well-developed inquiry program, and tries to build a social climate that encourages and supports individual inquiry of many kinds into many areas of life. The role of the staff members is to act as academic counselor to the children. Although the teachers have opinions about what would be productive for each child's personal inquiry, their teaching behavior is modulated to the students' frame of reference.

Independent Study

The student's independent study is at his or her own pace but toward goals held in common with other children in the group. For example, each student needs to learn word-attack skills in reading and in spelling, and the conventions of contemporary standard grammar. The self-instruction center offers many programs and materials each student can use independently as he or she works toward common goals at his or her own pace. A student may learn spelling through programmed instruction, arithmetic with a basal text and the help of a teacher, and phonics skills in a language laboratory. Progress is monitored through tests that are embedded in the instructional materials and scored by computers many miles from the school. The scores are interpreted by the teachers who have direct contact with the students, and they adjust each program according to the individual student's progress and learning style. Because some students have difficulty teaching themselves, the teachers stand ready to help them directly. For example, Marge met with several small groups in reading. Some students have difficulty learning to read by any means; others are readers of considerable capacity but find it difficult to learn through programmed or other self-instruction materials. One of Harvey's abilities is diagnosis of learning style and arrangement of environment so that the independent study programs are matched to the learner.

Each instruction team, however, tries to create a climate in which each student will take responsibility for his or her own learning. If a student has difficulty, the teacher acknowledges and helps the student to develop an independent study program designed to meet his or her problem.

Group Inquiry

People can teach themselves many things if they have a guide and a friend and the assistance of good books and other study materials. But some things are difficult to learn alone. It is no fun to debate the outcome of an election with yourself. Setting up hypotheses for an experiment often is better when the hypotheses must stand up against competition. Putting on a play is rarely a solitary endeavor. Discussion of important ideas is necessary if one's understanding is to be improved. So, students spend part of each day working within a small group, usually 5 to 10 children. These inquiry groups are formed at the beginning of the school year and changed as the year goes on. Their task is to determine areas of common interest. Teachers make many suggestions. For example, each year there is an inquiry about a political topic because such inquiry is considered essential to the education of each student. Some inquiries take only a few days; some take weeks or months.

The student also studies as a member of a large group — in these groups, lectures, simulations, and films are used as teaching vehicles. The purpose of such large-group study is to stimulate small-group inquiry. The direct-instruction team avoids large-group study for its own sake. If possible, lectures and demonstrations are videotaped so that small groups or individuals can observe them. Resource visitors are brought in to answer questions, rather than to lecture. If an information-giving session is scheduled, the direct-instruction team tries to get the visitor to tape record or videotape it.

Different students spend different amounts of time on personal inquiry, individual study, and group inquiry. Some individuals have such well-developed personal inquiry and individual study skills that the group learning of their education is rather small, and the opposite is true for others. However, the direct-instruction team tries to keep some balance in the life of each learner among all three modes of learning. Even a student who is having difficulty with personal inquiry may develop that skill if he or she has sufficient exposure to it and counseling. Every child can be taught to learn some things through individual study. At the other end of the spectrum are students who have trouble with group inquiry. This does not mean they should be withdrawn from it entirely, but that they may need special instruction in handling themselves as members of a group.

What we are saying here is that the child lives a balanced life as a learner. For personal inquiry, students study things that they select and that are important to them, but with assistance from their teachers. In independent study, they study subjects they understand will help them to develop in skill and in intellect. In group inquiry, they work with their peers, thrashing out what is significant and how to learn it.

Harvey does not work alone. He has staff support and the best technological aids the time we live in can provide. Furthermore, he is in a position to control technology — *he is not controlled by it.* Because his support centers have the capacity to create materials, Harvey is able to tailor the educational program to the needs of the child, the conditions in the community, and the nature of the academic disciplines.

MAKING THE DIMENSIONS OF EDUCATION EFFECTIVE

The students in Harvey Thompson's team in the Jefferson School engage in a variety of learning experiences that affect both the rate and the quality of their learning.

First, the overall social climate of the school supports specific values:

1. *An orientation toward achievement.* Students are expected to work hard and to push toward their highest level of achievment.
2. *Cooperation.* Students are expected to help one another and to value each other's differences as well as their similarities.
3. *Individual effort.* The school values each person's talents and generates a "you can do it" climate.
4. *Clarity of goals.* Each activity is explained to the children — they know what they are trying to learn and the entire staff works together to keep the goals clear.

Second, the school organization provides for individual differences. Students who are having difficulty receive personal attention, and those who are developing rapidly are given the opportunity to exploit their talents and to cover material quickly.

Each kind of instruction is carefully managed to ensure that the following criteria are met:

1. Diagnosis is linked to instruction. Every effort is made to teach students "where they are."
2. Activities build on one another to bring about cumulative effect.
3. Student work is monitored closely and students receive regular information about their achievement.
4. Teachers and staff relate to students in a positive way.

These are the elements that ensure student learning, whether we are creating new schools or tightening up the familiar old school around the corner.

JEFFERSON SCHOOL AND THE AVERAGE SCHOOL

The Jefferson School is not exotic, nor is it wildly futuristic. Most schools do some of the things described in the last few pages. However, the overall picture at Jefferson is quite different from that at most schools, because so many elements are smoothly combined, which allows the power of teachers and technologies to be harnessed and used appropriately. The differences between the Jefferson School and more conventional schools can be seen in the educational program, the organization of the conditions under which the staff works, and the ability of the staff to generate and receive innovations and to try them out.

The Program

The direct-instruction program embraces a wide range of objectives and each is used to support the others. Basic-skills instruction is individualized and closely monitored. The staff has several avenues through which they try to reach individual students. In this aspect of the program, the relationship between the students and the staff is similar to one's relationship with a personal physician: the clinician-teacher analyzes the state of the student's academic health and provides presciptions for self-administered therapy. If one course of treatment doesn't appear to be working, another is suggested. It is the patient, however, who must adhere to the regimen, and report in to have progress measured and to receive support.

Research and writing projects are generated by individual students and supported by the staff. Each student is expected to maintain one or more personal-inquiry projects. This type of relationship is like a client's relationship with a counselor. The teacher - counselor helps the student clarify goals and find the means to achieve them. Aides lend support as well, and the students also have the support centers to draw on. Each student is expected to learn how to use the tools that support inquiry — to employ computers, the library, filmed and taped courses and sources of information, and so on.

In cooperative inquiry, the teachers serve as instructors and as counselors to learning groups. Projects in the sciences, humanities, and social studies draw the students around problems to be solved and learning tasks to be accomplished. The teachers help them develop social and academic skills, and help them learn to support one another's efforts.

Because the resources are so rich, there are few limits on what students can strive to attain. Enormous sources of information and skills are available for both personal and group projects. In skill development, students are not held back "waiting" for their slower classmates, nor are they stymied because others progress faster.

The school does not try to achieve all of its goals through one method. The staff tries in several different fashions to help all students learn to learn, and believes that it will succeed with all children. It accepts differences, but also expects excellence from all.

Organization and Staffing

Perhaps the most striking thing about the Jefferson School is that teachers have time to plan both as individuals and as teams, and they have time to study what they teach and how they teach. They can specialize and yet learn from one another, shifting leadership according to what is being taught and how.

The support teams put Harvey and Marge's team in a powerful position. This team has vast resources to draw on as they create the educational program. Their students have access to printed, taped, filmed, and electronically stored information. With the help of the materials creation center, the staff can be creative in their approaches. They also have help in the diagnosis and prescription of learning needs and the monitoring of programs.

The direct-instruction teams are enriched by their aides and they are closely connected to their community. By involving community members in many roles, they can draw on the talent in their community — artists and scientists are invited to take teaching roles and the involvement of parents and others in shaping their program is encouraged.

Staff development is built into their job as team members study each other's teaching plans and help each other grow so that they can help their students gain access to a more powerful education.

The School Improvement Process

Possibly most striking, the Jefferson School direct-instruction team and its support centers make the process of improving the program, in ways large and small, a regular feature of life in the school. When a curriculum change is made, they can assemble the materials of instruction, receive training and instruction in academic content, and coach one another as they put the new curriculum in place.

The difference between Jefferson and the average school is in the number and degree of these features and the extent to which they are combined. In the average school teachers work alone for the most part, have access to fewer materials, and have little time to plan, alone or with others, let alone to engage in the reflective study that improvement of the program requires.

Yet nothing about Jefferson is exotic. All the conditions in that school can be generated for almost any school. What, then, is different about the conduct of education in schools such as Jefferson — schools that permit the assembly of materials and personnel into more productive forms than those employed in most schools?

CONDITIONS FOR SCHOOL IMPROVEMENT

When we describe schools such as Jefferson, or others that appear to have outstanding programs, the first question that comes usually is framed in the negative and may even be expressed in the declarative. Essentially, it is, "Well, you don't really expect us to bring an expensive plan like that to our public in these hard times, do you?" Turning the question somewhat, the answer is that the budget for a school like Jefferson probably would not be more than 10% higher than the average school budget. Perhaps a quarter of our schools today probably are adequately budgeted to do the job — were money the only facilitator. However, budgets must be reallocated, and additional money, when it is provided, must be managed in a way that will bring about a number of conditions.

First, to bring schools like Jefferson or any other vigorous model of the school into existence, the staff must have time for planning, preparation, study and materials development. If the workplace of the teacher does not change substantially, the generation of initiatives for substantial programmatic improvement will be very difficult. In the same way that reception of initiatives from outside the school is difficult when mastery of new ways of teaching or new academic content is required. The policy makers in Jefferson's district invested in the conditions that make rapid and solid school improvement possible.

Second, the leadership of Jefferson is bold and is not afraid to share power. Harvey, Marge, and the directors of the other teams and centers have great responsibility both for programs and for the development of their staffs, including aides and parent- tutors. The principal and the team and center leaders know how to build a facilitative and rigorous organizational climate that drives the continual improvement of the school and supports the development of staff members. They not only know how to teach, but also how to study teaching and how to teach others to teach. They are friends with academic content, technology, and the human needs of their co-workers and students.

The directors of the centers and the teams have had extensive education to prepare them for their roles. They have studied not only leadership, but technologies and models of teaching and curriculum development. They are supported by a hidden cadre of specialists in teaching, curriculum, and technology, from universities and from a coalition of school districts.

Jefferson school and the other schools in the same districts have school committees (what we will later call the *Responsible Parties*) that are responsible for examining the health of the school, for working with the teams to make alterations, and for communicating the program of the school and its needs to community members.

To return to an earlier question, "Is the community willing to invest in education and does it believe the investment will pay off handsomely for their children and the society as a whole?" The community insists on creative budgeting by the administration, but it can financially support the attempt to bring its children the best possible education.

Time, leadership, training, and community involvement have made it possible for the staff and the community to develop a shared understanding of their purposes and how to achieve them. In many schools, however, even mild improvements fall by the wayside, simply because the conditions of work do not allow the staff to develop the level of understanding that is needed to sustain coordinated school-improvement effort. Also, without public understanding and support, it is likely that any educational procedure that deviates from procedures in average schools will be viewed with suspicion by at least part of the community. The conditions necessary for improvement of the schools are provisions for planning and for continual study by the staff, strong and responsive leadership, access to rigorous training, redeployment of the staff, and close involvement of the community.

Jefferson shares another feature of our best schools: it is an assiduous borrower of ideas from others. Although the staff invent curriculum plans, teaching models, and instructional materials, most of the procedures and paraphernalia of education in Jefferson are adaptations of things and ideas developed elsewhere — in other districts, universities, research and development centers, and industries. The people who work in those places are another hidden cadre, backing up the efforts of the local school staff.

In the average school of today many powerful educational tools are underused or are not employed at all, because the conditions under which the staff works do not permit them to master these tools or to use them appropriately. Powerful curriculums, television, film, and computers all are underutilized. Most damaging of all, the human resources of the school are underutilized because provision is not made for their continued renewal, nor is provision made for giving teachers time for collective planning and individual preparation, for support services, and for the isolation of teachers' work stations.

III

DOWN-HOME
SCHOOL IMPROVEMENT

7

The Responsible Parties*

*Each local school needs a governing body
(we call it the Responsible Parties) — a
coalition of citizens, teachers, and school
administrators who constantly examine
the health of the school and make decisions
about how to improve it.*

We focus in this book on the *process* of school improvement. We
want our schools to be engaged in a constant process of
improvement. We want to see powerful mechanisms in place that
enable each school to deliver to the populations it serves the most
vigorous kind of education it is possible to offer. Education is an
enterprise so large and so complex that the problem of improving
it tends to baffle even the best minds. School improvement
actually boils down to an attempt to improve the society itself. It
means persuading a lot of people to support processes that will
lead to improved education, or at least persuading them not to
stand in the way of people who do have ideas and energy to devote
to the task. A school improvement program must be very broad
and yet it must be guided by a few straightforward ideas, or else
the effort will be diffused in the welter of social currents that swirl
around the school. We will concentrate on a few propositions we

*For detailed description of grass-roots school improvement see: Joyce, Hersh, and
McKibbin (1983).

think should be guiding principles in school reform efforts. These propositions do not represent an ideological position on what constitutes a good education. We think they can be used by proponents of numerous points of view — proponents of student-centered education, academic-centered education, education for the minorities and the handicapped — because these propositions are not designed to produce a particular type of education, but to generate a process for helping people choose the kind of education they want. Most of these propositions focus on the process of improving the local school, but some, of necessity, address the development of conditions that will enable local schools to flourish.

A COMMITTEE OF RESPONSIBLE PARTIES

Who are these people who are to be responsible for the direction of the school? They should be drawn from several sources:

1. *Representatives of the general public.* Local boards of education are the most common means of controlling education in public schools in the United States. However, state legislatures and boards of education, departments of public instruction, and other agencies frequently exercise some direction over schools. Sometimes they issue general regulations or policies within which schools may operate. In other situations (especially those in which there are local boards of education in small communities), state or regional service agencies may become intimately involved with shaping the school. However, local boards often give great latitude to privately financed schools, requiring only compliance with health regulations and building maintenance standards. In any case, representatives of the general public should be involved in determining the direction of a school program.

2. *Site administrators and representatives of the school district administration.* As early as possible in the develop-

ment of a new school program — or in the regeneration of an existing one — designated officials should be given the executive functions they need to see the planning through and to bring new schools into existence. Whenever possible, officials expected to work in the new school program should be included in this group. Throughout the planning process these individuals are expected to procure the expert assistance the program planners will need. However, the site and district administrators need not see themselves as the "directors" of the school, in the superficial meaning of that term, because the plan for the school might call for a nondirective form of leadership or even self-government by the students.

3. *Teachers.* The planning group should include teachers with the capacity to envision new and alternative educational forms. Such teachers represent our accumulated knowledge about the educational process. Representatives of the public usually have limited views of educational possibilities (although in some communities they exceed the professional staff in this respect), whereas leading teachers are students of the educational process. As planning moves toward the development of implementation strategies, the instructional specialists will need to play a larger leadership role in shaping specific components of the school and bringing it into existence.

4. *Technical consultants.* Because it is unlikely that the individuals in any local situation will possess among themselves all the expert knowledge that will be needed, the Responsible Parties must bring into the planning process specialists in curriculum planning, educational technology, architecture, and school administration. The types of competency needed will become apparent as we describe the tasks involved in creating a model for a school.

5. *Patrons of the school.* The Responsible Parties should include parents and children, especially in large school districts, where school boards and other public representatives are likely to be quite remote. Children

should not be involved in all aspects of planning, but should react to ideas when the child's view seems important.

Imagine a committee that is charged with the task of creating a school. It includes representatives of the public, school officials, teachers, technological experts, parents, and children. The committee might be set up by the legally Responsible Parties. If a private school corporation is initiating the school, the corporation can set up the committee. If a board of education is responsible, it can determine the membership or set in motion the machinery for assembling it. Or, a school committee might be assembled by people who hope to influence educational practice, although they have no legal authority themselves. For instance, a firm of architects might decide to develop school models and, in the process, might assemble a representative body, including members of the public, for reality-testing purposes. Similarly, a group of technologists planning a school might include administrators and parents, not out of any political motive but simply to test the viability for potential customers of their model.

Building Collaborative Local Governance

The first task is to build a social context that involves everyone concerned with the school (the Responsible Parties). The object of bringing together the Responsible Parties is to build a community that can continuously rethink the purposes of the school, select its primary mission, choose its most appropriate operating methods, evaluate how they work, make adjustments, and, over time, repeat this cycle.

By providing ways for community members, teachers, and administrative staff to participate in the creation of the educational program, the Responsible Parties can ensure that the following goals are met:

1. The school program is intelligible to everyone concerned.
2. Conflict over alternatives is resolved, or at least dealt with, in a manner that prevents disgruntled factions from subverting the program.

3. There is support for the new program and debate is open and reasonable.
4. There is coordination among administrators, teachers, and community members.

In other words, the Responsible Parties need to assemble a community that deliberately and openly builds, supports, evaluates, and rethinks the school program. If administrators initiate change without involving teachers, little real change is likely to occur. If teachers generate ideas but the administration is uncommitted to them, any idea is likely to remain just that — a thought. If the community does not understand or approve a change in the program, it is likely to be short-lived.

The solution is to build a continuous program-rethinking process that includes representatives of all three groups. This is not to suggest that the entire school program will be changed each year! Making changes is difficult even when there is broad involvement and firm agreement about what is to done. As the Responsible Parties study the school they will develop priorities for change, and the efforts of any given year will be concentrated on the high-priority objectives.

The practice of rethinking the school's missions and means must become embedded in the life of the school and its community; the search for improvement must become a normal process; the atmosphere in which it occurs must encourage serious reflection and discourage excessive advocacy. Fresh ideas that are put forth dogmatically draw defensive reactions ("What's wrong with the way we are doing things now?").

Innovations nearly always stumble at first. A faculty must experiment with the introduction of new content into the curriculum. The first experiments often are awkward. In a climate that is harsh and unforgiving of error, the period of trial and experimentation will not succed in allowing new methods to be massaged into comfortable processes.

In the early 1960s, as the academic reform movement propelled new mathematics and science content into the elementary and secondary schools, nearly everyone became uncomfortable, and an angry and panicky climate arose. Teachers were learning the governing principles of operations with integers and rational numbers. It was alleged that the new mathematics content would undermine the learning of basic facts. Teachers who were weak in science became insecure. Administrators watched apprehensively as content they did not understand poured into their schools. Parents worried about helping their children with Venn diagrams and Cartesian multiplication. Children labored with "structure and function" in biology. Although these new curriculums were well thought-out in most cases and were backed up with excellent instructional materials, implementation was difficult because these programs rarely became part of the ongoing culture of the school community.

Clearly, if the interested groups — community, faculty, and administration — are carefully involved in the adoption and adaptation of curriculum plans, many of the problems just described can be avoided. Broad governance of the school will not guarantee smooth sailing, but it is an essential element in the strategy of school improvement. Pro forma involvement is insufficient. The Responsible Parties must develop what we call *parity* — relative equality among teachers, community, and administration. The experiment in participatory governance of local schools (described in Joyce, Hersh, & McKibbin [1983], Ch. 10) illustrates the concept of parity. In this case, the school community councils of the Urban/Rural Program were nearly two years in development before they began to function effectively! The Responsible Parties can build such parity-oriented governance systems, but it takes time.

School Improvement Programs

A Climate of Support. Collaborative governance provides for broad involvement and generates a forum for rational debate about the ends and means of the school. The Responsible Parties select objectives that will be the focus for innovation in the school program. One of the most important elements in a successful school improvement program is a social climate that supports people as they formulate ideas and try them out on the school staff.

As stated previously, putting educational ideas to work is difficult and frustrating. Consider the example of a school where many students feel poorly about themselves as learners. The Responsible Parties decide to attack the problem. They decide to experiment with teaching strategies designed to boost the students' feelings of adequacy and self-esteem. Teachers organize workshops to study those strategies and how to use them. When the time to try them out arrives, the new strategies at first feel awkward to the teachers, and students have difficulty responding to them. Parents worry that their children aren't learning enough. Administrators worry about discipline. All of these reactions are quite normal. What is important, however, is what happens next, and that depends to a considerable extent on the social climate that is generated among community, teachers, and adminstrators.

If everyone understands what is going on, lends support, and helps one another over the rough spots, we can predict that the awkward period will ease, and everyone involved will become comfortable with the new approach; students will respond and parents and administrators will relax. However, if the climate is harsh and unforgiving, if mistakes are not tolerated, if the atmosphere becomes heated with anxiety, then we can predict that discouragement and anxiety will prevail. Within such a negative atmosphere the new approach will soon give way to the old as teachers return to the safe and familiar ways that aroused few complaints, even if they caused children to feel bad about themselves.

During the 1970s, The Rand Corporation study team (Berman & McLaughlin, 1975) came to conclusions similar to ours. They found that organizations that sucessfully implemented agreed-upon changes developed vertical as well as horizontal integration. In terms of school organization, this means that the school board, the central administration of the district, the building administrators, the teachers, and the community members must all work in concert. For example, a local school group working without support from the central administration or the school board will soon get into difficulty; a school board and central administration that fails to include local community members and teachers in their organization will be equally doomed.

Although the contrast between "top-down" and "bottom-up" initiatives for change receives a lot of attention these days, it appears that change can be initiated equally well from either direction. Regardless of who presents the initiative, vertical integration of the various levels of the system is essential.

The Rand Corporation study team also found that a supportive organizational climate is vital. Innovation involves risk taking. Unless a climate exists that supports risk-taking behavior or at least avoids punishing experimentation, we can hardly expect people to feel encouraged to take the first fumbling steps that are essential as innovations are tried out. A supportive climate is an essential element of the school improvement strategy.

8

Investment in People through Staff Development Programs

Creating training programs on an ad hoc basis whenever a curriculum change is made would be horrendously expensive and disruptive. The kind of training we propose must be embedded in the lives of teachers. If the education profession is to flourish and if schools are to be a vital force in society, it is necessary to rebuild the school into a lifelong learning laboratory, not only for children but for teachers as well. The improvement of staff development programs is not simply a matter of deciding how to create and implement ad hoc programs. Rather, it is a broad endeavor aimed at generating a rich environment, one in which every educator becomes a student of education and works continuously to improve his or her skills. The environment of the school must regenerate the relationships between teachers, learners, and community members, or the school will lose its vitality.

Making schools into learning laboratories will be a long, slow process, but it is time for us to make the commitment and to put our energies into that process, and not waste them by repeating the mistakes of the past. *The primary task in staff development is to develop an ecology in all schools that nurtures professional growth.* The purposes are three:

1. To enrich the lives of teachers and administrators so that they continuously expand their general education, their emotional range, and their understanding of children.

2. To generate continuous efforts to improve schools. School faculties, administrators, and community members need to work together to acquire the knowledge and skills necessary to bring those improvements into existence.

3. To create conditions that enable professional skill development to be continuous. All teachers and administrators must be students of learning and teaching and engage in a continuous process of experimentation with their own behavior and that of their students. They need to study alternative approaches to schooling and teaching, to select ones that will expand their capabilities, and to acquire the understanding and skills necessary to make fresh alternatives a part of their ongoing professional repertoire.

It is quite clear that curriculum implementation and instructional improvement are very difficult unless a strong staff development program is in place. If teachers and community members do not achieve *their* own needed learning, it will be impossible for the students to do so. It is equally clear that effective methods for staff development exist, and that such programs can be implanted in the ongoing operation of the school. To do so is, in itself, to bring about a major change in the social sytem of education. Without this kind of staff development, new curriculums cannot be implemented and faculty will have extreme difficulty working together to make instructional improvements.

We want to stress that implementation of all but the most mild changes *requires* training in content or process. The findings of research on curriculum implementation are unequivocal: very little implementation will take place, even in positive environments or by highly motivated people, *unless* training is provided (Fullan & Pomfret, 1977; Hall & Loucks, 1977; Joyce et al., 1981). Thus, strong and regular training is an essential aspect of an environment favorable to school improvement. Such training must be far more extensive and intricate than what is provided in most professional environments today.

TRAINING TO ENSURE TRANSFER

The question is: What kinds of training do teachers need in order to implement new curriculum plans?

Let us examine another scenario. This time a team of teachers is using research-based techniques for learning a new teaching strategy.

The eight members of the English department of Lazarus High School are studying new teaching strategies they are considering for use in some of their courses. The model of teaching currently on their agenda is Synectics (Gordon, 1961), designed to stimulate metaphoric thinking. Several members of the department think Synectics will be a useful strategy to encourage creative writing and also in the study of fiction and poetry. They began their exploration by reading Gordon's book *Synectics.* Next, an expert on the strategy came to the school, demonstrated it several times, and held discussions with them. They also saw a videotaped lecture of Gordon explaining the theory on which Synectics is based, and visited a school where two teachers have been using Synectics for the past two or three years. The next step was to plan little lessons based on the Synectics procedure and to try them out on one another. They taught each other lessons in creative writing and in the analysis of poetry. They examined the use of metaphor in Ionesco's plays. Each teacher practiced the teaching strategy several times with the other teachers before trying it out with students. Then, working in teams of two, they began to try out the strategy, first with the most able students in their elective writing classes. One team member taught and the other offered constructive criticism, then they switched places. Sometimes they taught together. Each practiced several times with the "coaching partner" present to reflect on progress and to offer suggestions about how to improve the next trial.

Then, still working in teams, they began to work the teaching strategy into a few of their courses, using it in places where it seemed it to be the most productive and where they were highly likely to have success. Not surprisingly, they found that the hardest part of using a new model of teaching is not learning what to do as a teacher, but teaching the students to relate to the model. For example, the Synectics strategy asks the students to generate "personal analogies," such as imagining themselves to be a snowman, tennis ball, dinosaur, lawnmower, toothbrush, etc. A few of the students were puzzled by the instruction to "be a toothbrush and describe how you feel and what you think about your users." It took time before some of the kids tuned into the procedures and became comfortable with them. Also, some of the variations of the Synectics model asked the students to share their writing publicly — at best an uncomfortable procedure for some of the students.

As time passed the Lazarus team found it useful to reread parts of Gordon's book and to revisit the teachers who were more experienced users of Synectics. They were fortunate to obtain the consultative services of a Synectics expert for a day. She reviewed the theory and gave them some tips for practicing and coaching one another.

The Lazarus team is engaged in the serious study of alternative models to teaching (Joyce & Weil, 1980) and is using training procedures that are virtually guaranteed to bring most approaches to teaching within its grasp.

Over the years (Joyce & Showers, 1983) we have accumulated a number of research reports on how teachers learn to integrate a new approach into their active repertoire. Studying theory, observing demonstrations, and practicing with feedback are sufficient to enable most teachers to develop their skills to the point where they can use a model fluidly and appropriately when called on to do so. Skill development by itself, however, does not ensure transfer. Relatively few persons who obtain skill in new approaches to teaching will make that skill a part of their regular practice, unless they receive additional instruction. Not until the coaching component is added into the equation and used effectively, will most teachers begin to transfer their model into their active repertoire.*

The first message we are able to summarize from this research is very positive: teachers are wonderful learners. Nearly all teachers can acquire new skills that "fine tune" their competence. They also can learn a considerable repertoire of teaching strategies that are new to them.

The second message is more sobering, but still optimistic. In order to improve their skills and learn new approaches to teaching, teachers need conditions that are not commonly found in most in-service settings, even when teachers participate in governance of those settings.

The third message, also very encouraging, is that the research base reveals what conditions help teachers to learn. This information can be used in designing appropriate staff development activities for classroom personnel.

Components of Training

Most of the training literature describes investigations in which training elements are combined in various ways — some combinations focus on the fine tuning of styles, and others focus on the mastery of new approaches. In our analysis we identified a number of training components that have been studied intensively. Alone and in combination, each of these training components contributes to the impact of a training sequence or activity. (As we shall see, when individual components are combined, each has much greater power than when used alone.) The five major components of training we found in the studies we reviewed are as follows:

1. *Presentation of theory.* Studying theory can provide the rationale, conceptual base, and verbal description of an approach to teaching or instructional technique. Readings, lectures, films, and discussions are among the most common

---

*Transfer of new items of repertoire is more than the transfer of skills that polish or "fine tune" models of teaching that lie within the existing repertoire.

forms of presentation. In many higher education courses and in-service institutes and workshops, presentation of theory often is the major, and in some cases, the sole component of the training experience. In research on training, study of theory frequently is combined with one or more of the other components.

Level of impact. Whether the goal is fine tuning of style or mastery of new approaches, presentation of theory can raise awareness and increase conceptual control of an aspect of teaching. However, presentation of theory rarely results in skill acquisition or the transfer of skills into the classroom situation (although some people are able to build and transfer skills from theory presentations alone). On the other hand, when theory is used in combination with other training components, it appears to boost conceptual control, skill development, and transfer.

2. *Modeling or demonstration.* Modeling involves enactment of a teaching skill or strategy, through either a live demonstration with children or adults or through demonstrations presented via television, film, or other media. In a given training activity, a strategy or skill can be modeled any number of times. Much of the literature on modeling is flawed, because only one or two demonstrations of some quite complex models of teaching are available.

Level of impact. Modeling appears to have a considerable effect on awareness and some effect on knowledge. Demonstration also increases mastery of theory — in other words, we understand better what is illustrated to us. Many teachers can initiate demonstrated skills fairly readily, and a number will transfer them to classroom practice. However, for most teachers, modeling alone is unlikely to result in the acquisition and transfer of skills unless it is accompanied by other components. When fine tuning of style is the goal, a fairly good level of impact can be achieved through the use of modeling alone, but for mastering new approaches it does not by itself have great power for many teachers. All in all, research indicates that modeling very likely is an important component of any training program aimed at acquisition of complex skills and their transfer to the classroom situtation.

3. *Practice under simulated conditions.* Practice involves trying out a new skill or strategy. Simulated conditions usually are achieved by practicing either with peers or with small groups of children under circumstances in which the teacher does not have to manage an entire class or a larger group of children at the same time.

Level of impact. It is difficult to practice without prior awareness and knowledge; that is, we have to know what it is we are to practice. However, when awareness and knowledge have been achieved, practice is a very efficient way of acquiring skills and strategies related to the tuning of style or to the mastery of new approaches. Once a relatively high level of skill has been achieved, a sizable percentage of teachers will begin to transfer the skill into their instructional situations. It is probable that the more complex and unfamiliar the skill or strategy is, the lower will be the level of transfer. Research supports common sense about practice under simulated conditions. That is, it is an extremely effective way to develop competence in a wide variety of classroom techniques.

4. *Structured feedback.* Structured feedback involves learning a system for observing teaching behavior, and providing an opportunity to reflect on those observations. Feedback can be self-administered, provided by observers, or given by peers and coaches; it can be regular or occasional. Structured feedback can be combined with other components — for example, it can be directly combined with practice, and a practice-feedback-practice sequence can be developed.

Level of impact. Feedback alone can produce considerable awareness of one's teaching behavior and knowledge about alternatives. With respect to the fine tuning of styles, it is a reasonably powerful strategy for acquiring skills and transferring them to the classroom situation. For example, if feedback is given about patterns of rewarding and punishing, many teachers will begin to modify the ways they reward and punish children. Similarly, if feedback is provided about the kinds of questions asked in the classroom, many teachers will become more aware of their use of questions and will set goals for changes. In general, these changes persist as long as feedback continues, but when it stops, teaching styles gradually slide back toward their original point. In other words, feedback alone does not appear to provide permanent changes, but in many areas of behavior regular and consistent feedback is probably necessary if people are to make and maintain changes in those behaviors.

5. *Coaching for application.* When training components are used in combination, the levels of impact are considerable for most teachers up through the skill level, whether the object is the fine tuning of style or the mastery of new approaches to teaching. For example, for nearly all (probably 9 out of 10) teachers at the in-service or pre-service levels, the skill-acquisition level of impact is reached when demonstration of unfamiliar models of teaching or curriculum approaches is combined with discussions of theory and followed by practice with structured feedback. If consistent feedback combined with classroom practice is provided, a good many, but not all, will transfer their skills into the teaching situation. For many others, however, direct coaching on how to apply the new skills and models appears to be necessary. Coaching can be provided by colleagues, supervisors, professors, curriculum consultants, or others thoroughly familiar with the new approaches. Coaching involves helping teachers analyze the content to be taught and the approach to be taken, and making very specific plans to help the student adapt to the new teaching approach.

For maximum effectiveness in most in-service training activities, it appears that the most effective course is to include several, and perhaps all, of the five training components. Where fine tuning of style is the goal, modeling, practice under simulated conditions, and practice in the classroom combined with feedback, probably will result in considerable improvement. Where mastery of a new approach is the desired outcome, both presentations and discussions of theory and coaching probably are necessary as well. If the theory of a new approach is well presented, the approach is demonstrated, practice is provided under simulated conditions with careful and consistent feedback, and that practice is followed by application in the classroom with coaching and further feedback, it is likely that the vast majority of teachers will be able to expand their repertoire to utilize a wide variety of approaches to teaching and curriculum. If any of these components are left out, the impact of training will be weakened because fewer people will progress to the transfer level (which is the only level that has significant meaning for school improvement).

The most effective training activities, then, will be those that combine theory, modeling, practice, feedback, and coaching for application. A reasonably firm knowledge base underlies our prediction that we can expect outcomes to be considerable at all levels, if these five components are in fact combined in in-service programs.

We have learned that skill development alone will not bring about transfer. We understand that after a teaching skill is learned it must be adapted, because classroom situations are different from training situations. One cannot simply walk from the training session into the classroom with a new skill completely ready to use. For a teacher to use the skill apppropriately and forcefully in its context, he or she must have a clear understanding of the students, the subject matter, the objectives, and the classroom management variables.

All of us are less skillful with a new model of teaching than we are with existing ones. For successful transfer to occur, one needs a period of time in which to practice the skill in its context, until it is as finely tuned as elements of one's existing repertoire. Sometimes, however, sets of teaching behaviors that support the existing repertoire may inhibit implementation of new models of teaching. We see this, for example, when a teacher accustomed to running brisk and pointed drill and practice sessions begins to learn how to work inductively with students. The swift pace of the drill and practice, the directive feedback to the students, and the ability to control the content and movement of the lesson are somewhat dysfunctional as the teacher becomes less directive, relies more on initiative from the students, probes their understanding, and helps them learn to give one another feedback. The new teaching strategy seems awkward at first. Its pace seems slow. The teaching moves that served so well before now appear to retard the new kind of lesson. After a while, practice in context smooths off rough edges and the teacher gradually comes to feel as comfortable with the new strategy and as much in control of it as he or she felt with the old one.

In summary, three elements in addition to coaching are needed to deal with the transfer problem (or, really, to prevent a transfer problem):

- Forecasting the transfer process throughout the training cycle
- Reaching the highest possible level of skill development during training
- Developing what we call *executive control;* that is, an understanding of the appropriate content for the model and how to adapt it to students of varying characteristics — a "metaunderstanding" of how the model works, which can be fitted into the instructional repertoire and adapted to students

PARALLELS WITH ATHLETIC TRAINING

We are beginning to discover parallels between the problem of transfer in teaching and the problem of transfer in athletic skills.

There are going to be so many things in your head that your muscles just aren't going to respond like they should for awhile... You've got to understand that the best way to get through this is to relax, not worry about your mistakes, and come to each practice and each meeting anxious to learn. *We'll generally make you worse before we make you better.**

Coach Brooks's recent admonition to his freshmen high-lights the parallels. Intrigued, I approached Coach Brooks and

*Coach Rich Brooks of the University of Oregon to his incoming freshmen football players, in *The Eugene Register-Guard,* August 14, 1981.

asked him to talk with me about athletic training and the problems of transfer. My interview with him revealed striking similarities in the training problems faced by teachers, football players, and their coaches.

Q. Coach Brooks, I'm interested in how you approach skill development in football training and if you consider the transfer of those skills to game conditions to be a separate training problem.

A. Although our players come to us with skills, we reteach and refine these skills as though we were starting from scratch. We teach them our way of doing it, because all those skills have to fit together into one team. They're all interdependent.

Q. Could you tell me your approach to skill development?

A. We use a part/whole/part method. All skills are broken down into discrete steps. We work each segment, then combine them into whole skills, then into plays, etc., then go back and work on the specifics of skills that are giving problems.

Q. Could you give me an example of a specific skill and how you would approach the training for that skill?

A. The fundamentals of blocking and tackling—bending the knees and striking a blow. All positions need this skill. The trick is to get the player to visualize, to have a mental picture of how it looks and how it feels. Otherwise feedback isn't effective. We can tell them where it's wrong, but they can't correct it till they know.

Q. How do you get them "to know" what the skill is?

A. We tell them, show them, demonstrate with people and with film, show them films of themselves, have them practice with the [word(s) indecipherable].

Q. The what?

A. It's a mechanical dummy they practice with. We have them practice each move seperately, then put the moves together, first one, then two, then three — how their knees should be bent, where their arms should come up, where they strike, what all the muscles should be doing. We diagnose problems with the dummy and keep explaining how it should work, over and over again, in sequence.

Q. In teacher training, we believe that theoretical understanding is important to later performance. How important is it in football skills?

A. It's essential. They must understand how their bodies work, why certain muscles in certain combinations achieve certain effects. We never stop explaining.

Q. After they have mastered blocking to your satisfaction with the dummy, then what?

A. Moving from the machine to a live test is difficult; moving from practice to a game is also very difficult. Some people have all the physical ability in the world, all the moves, but can't play because they can't grasp the entire concept, can't fit in with the whole picture.

Q. We have problems with transfer of training, too. Do you coach them differently after they've mastered the "basic skills" of football? What will you be doing differently next month after the season has started? How do you work on transfer?

A. Fear of failure is a factor. My job is to create confidence and success situations. Skills have to be overlearned so that they're past conscious thinking. I can't have someone thinking of how to throw a block in a game. They have to be thinking of who and when and what the guy on their left or behind them is doing.

Q. So specifically, how do you coach transfer of skills to a game situation?

A. First, we re-emphasize skill training for everyone — the second, third, fourth year guys as well. We're always working for improved execution. Then we work hardest on integration, which is just a new kind of teaching. Coaching is really just teaching. We work on confidence by putting them in situations where they can see the improvement. If a guy was lifting 300 pounds two weeks ago and is lifting 350 now, no one has to tell him he's getting stronger.

Q. How does the training break down for your players right now, before school starts?

A. We spend 3 hours in the classroom and 2 hours on the field. On their own, they spend a couple of hours in the weight room and working out, and another couple of hours with the trainers, working out their bumps and bruises.

Q. And after school starts?

A. We'll spend 45 minutes a day in class, 2 hours on the practice field, plus whatever they can manage on their own after studies.

Q. How does that differ from the pro football players' training regimen?

A. They meet 2-3 hours daily in position meetings, offensive and defensive meetings, watching films of themselves and their opponents, then practice 2 to 4 hours a day depending on their coaches, then their personal work and time with the trainers. They have more time to get into the complexities of the game.

Changing what we do, even slightly, can unbalance the rest of our "game." Whether we are adjusting the grip on a golf club or initiating an inquiry procedure for science teaching, the new behavior does not fit smoothly with our existing behaviors. The fact that the new skill may have been perfected in parts and practiced thoroughly in simulated conditions does not prevent the transfer problem. Behaviors that surround the new skill must be adjusted to the presence of a different approach, and the resulting discomfort often is enough to ensure a return to the former smooth, if less efficient, performance.

Perhaps the most striking difference in training between athletes and teachers is the initial assumptions held by each. *Athletes do not believe mastery will be achieved quickly or easily.* They understand that enormous effort will result in small (and not always linear) increments of change. We, on the other hand, often behave as though teaching skills are so easily acquired that a simple presentation, a one-day workshop, or a single videotaped demonstration are sufficient to ensure successful classroom performance. To the extent that we have communicated this message to teachers, we have misled them. Learning to use an inductive strategy in the classroom surely is at least as difficult as learning to throw a block properly.

Coach Brooks's description parallels the argument I have tried to make. The task of learning new skills and integrating them, the knowledge that "we'll generally make you worse before we make you better," and the importance of continuing to try when the results are discouraging eloquently forecast the transfer process. The need to overlearn skills to the point where they become automatic, if they are to be useful in a more complex setting, is also reflected in Brooks's training regimen. "Executive control" is sought in the frequent and ongoing emphasis on theory and in the classsroom work on "plays," "game plans," and analysis of films.

The elements of coaching in teaching — the provision of championship and technical feedback, study of application, study of students (or opposing teams), and personal facilitation — are clear in the interview with Coach Brooks. Football players, however, have a built-in advantage when undertaking the training process: their training is *organized* as a group activity with continuous feedback from coaches. I came away from this interview feeling more strongly than ever that teachers also must organize themselves into groups for the express purpose of training themselves and each other and to facilitate the transition from skill development to transfer.

INVESTING IN PEOPLE

Why do I discuss at such great length what it takes to help teachers learn new approaches to teaching? The answer is this: unless the investment in staff development is vastly increased over its present level, school improvement of any kind simply will not take place. As I have said several times, only 3 to 4 work days per year are currently allotted to staff develoment, and less than 10% of this time includes training that is as thoroughgoing as the training we have described. *The reason so many promising curriculum and technological innovations have not been adequately implemented is very simple: the accompanying training has been inadequate.*

All successful enterprises invest in their personnel: In the military, of course, personnel train *all* the time. In high technology industries, it is not unusual for technicians, engineers, middle managers, and salespeople to train for 30-50 days per year. (You simply cannot sell expensive mainframe computers unless you understand them and their uses.) Even in some homely occupations, the amount of time invested is considerable. I recently discovered that the officers of my bank receive 3 days of training each month (12 times what the average teacher receives). My hair dresser studies new styles, cosmetics, and techniques for 10 days each year. Each year my accountant takes a 2-week update on changes in the tax code. My auto mechanic attends 10 to 15 days of classes each year. The teachers of my children have 3 or 4 days of training each year.

Furthermore, none of these people work in isolation. They can consult with their colleagues when they need to. And they have time, when appropriate, to plan together and to attend meetings called by managers.

Teachers are analogous to actors who are asked to give 6 performances each day without rehearsal. It is no wonder that many of them repeat the same acts a little too often.

The workplace must change: a much larger investment must be made in helping teachers increase the strength of what they presently do. Without such changes, it will not be possible to make the improvements we now envision for our schools.

9

Refinement, Renovation, Redesign

Three levels of school improvement must be established. The first refinement of the present operation. The second in renovation of aspects of the program. The third is redesign to accommodate new technological and staffing systems.

Schools, like other social organizations, are not disposed toward change, and from that fact emerges an important paradox that provides a clue to the solution to the problem. The paradox is quite simple: schools seek stability as a seemingly necessary condition of survival. Yet this condition of equilibrium is also the root cause of the school's inability to improve, for as society changes and/or pedogogical knowledge increases, schools need to assimilate and accommodate new realities. How can a school create a reasonable level of stability and also constantly be open and able to change?

The answer lies in the creation of a certain type of school culture — a set of organizational norms, expectations, beliefs, and behaviors that allow the establishment of activities fundamental to school improvement. This means that what must remain constant, what must remain stable in the life of the school, is an emotional and intellectual disposition on the part of

Responsible Parties toward improvement. We call this condition *homeostasis of improvement.*

All schools can improve. My task in this book is to explain how such improvment takes place, to specify the particulars of the process. *I identify three stages of school improvement — refinement, renovation, and redesign — the three Rs.* In identifying and describing each of the stages of purposeful and evolutionary school improvement, I focus on the structural relationships among the various organizational elements.

Describing a process of school improvement is only part of my task, however. As schools increase their capacity to manage their growth they must also constantly reconsider the purposes of their existence. It is through this more fundamental pre/reviewing of their function that school organizations achieve a capacity to accept the necessity of continual growth as a condition of organizational survival.

THE THREE Rs OF SCHOOL IMPROVEMENT

In order to make school improvement a way of life, I envision three successive stages of growth. In Stage 1, criteria from research on effective schools are used to refine the current operation of the school. Curriculum and instructional practices are examined and sets of refinements developed to make them more effective. We are not changing the animal, but we are grooming it, slimming it down, giving it more exercise. It is the same beast, but it works better. In Stage 2, the organization matures — it examines curriculum areas in more depth and selects specific components of its program to be systematically improved by innovation. New content and teaching strategies are introduced at this point, along with increasing amounts and types of staff development. In Stage 3, the overall mission of the school is examined and the entire range of curricular and instructional options is considered. Table 9.1 illustrates the three stages of school improvement.

During each phase we will be building a sound organization, establishing effective training, and making productive change a regular feature of the school.

TABLE 9.1. THREE STAGES OF SCHOOL IMPROVEMENT

		Scope	*Tasks*
Stage 1:	Refine	Initiate the process	Organize Responsible Parties Use effective criteria Improve social climate of education
Stage 2:	Renovate	Establish the process	Expand scope of improvement Embed staff development Improve curriculum areas
Stage 3:	Redesign	Expand the scope	Examine mission of school Study technologies Scrutinize organizational structure Develop long-term plan

Building a Sound Organization

As I have said before, collaborative governance takes time to develop. People must learn to work together, become familiar with the available models of schooling, choose among them. and mobilize to implement their decisions. Judging from the experience of the Urban/Rural Program (Joyce, Hersh, McKibbin, 1983), councils of Responsible Parties require a maturation period of about two years, during which time procedures for making decisions and a common knowledge base are developed. During this period the Responsible Parties may need assistance from consultants in both *process* (how to work together effectively) and *substance* (what are the options and how can they be implemented).

The maturation period is extremely important. The Responsible Parties must avoid making decisions that would radically change the character of the school before they have acquired an adequate knowledge of alternatives and implementation problems. A large number of alternatives exist and it takes time to become educated consumers of them. Also, it is wise not to attempt radical change at first. Until the decision-making process is well established and resources are adequately mobilized, changes should be minor. The Responsible Parties can select a single curriculum area and work on it, learning how to make decisions cooperatively and how to make small changes happen. This is an ideal activity for the maturation period.

Louis Smith (Smith & Keith, 1971) has provided a wonderful study of a group of talented administrators and teachers who attempted a quick, radical change of an entire school program. They had to retrain themselves, develop community support, assemble instructional materials, and deal with their critics — all within the space of a few months. The new program came awkwardly into existence, was the focus of angry social ferment, and was eroded within a year. By taking our time and learning by degrees we can have a reasonable chance of avoiding the kind of experiences Smith describes.

Building Effective Training

Nearly every worthwhile educational change includes changes in the use of instructional strategies. Teachers and students alike have to take on new patterns of behavior. Consider the example of a science curriculum designed on the premise that students should learn to think inductively — to collect and analyze data, build and test hypotheses, and generate concepts for organizing information. To implement such a design requires inductive learning processes, which in turn require teaching strategies by which teachers demonstrate to students how to think inductively.

As indicated previously, the curriculum implementation literature indicates quite clearly that unless very intensive staff training accompanies a curriculum change in content or in teaching process, the level of implementation will be very low (Fullan & Pomfret, 1977). Put positively, training is essential. Teachers can provide much of the training for one another, but they must be provided the time and opportunity to do so.

Making Change Familiar

In most communities, educational change has been a nervous, controversial process attempted on an inadequate social and technical base. Innovation in education will remain uncomfortable — and largely unsuccessful — until we build communities of laymen and professionals who will take the time to plan realistically and mobilize powerfully. Until the goal of continual school improvement becomes a familiar and regular feature of the educational scene, innovations will last only as long as forceful people hold them together. Resistance to change is natural. Only when citizens and educators regularly and comfortably institute changes, when the improvement of schools becomes familiar and normal, will innovations become as natural as resistance to it is at present.

STAGE 1

Assume that a committee of Responsible Parties has been formed and is just starting to work. What do they do? At the risk of being too specific, we set forth the following 12 tasks for them to engage in at the Stage 1 improvement level.

1. Organize the Responsible Parties to study the school program and environment.
2. Develop relationships among the community, district, administration, sources of technical assistance, and the council.
3. Commence studying the school using the effectiveness criteria.
4. Select a focus for improvement.
5. Assemble the necessary resources.
6. Provide time for training.
7. Communicate, communicate, and communicate.
8. Prepare the pilot study.
9. Carry out the pilot study.
10. Revise the innovation.
11. Commence implementation.
12. Evaluate and fine tune the innovation.

Let us now examine each task in turn.

Task 1: Organize the Responsible Parties to study the school program and environment. At the beginning stages, the organization and functioning of the Responsible Parties will require considerable time and effort. The school administrators and the faculty need to meet and determine a method for electing or appointing members to a school-community council that will be the exclusive committee of the Responsible Parties. This council then needs to call a community meeting to explain its purpose and to discuss methods of securing representation from the community. In some communities the Parent-Teacher Association (PTA) can take on much of the responsibility for developing community representation, but in other communities the activities of the PTA are probably best confined to teacher-parent relationships.

In complex communities it is probably wise to establish a pro tem council responsible for establishing a method that insures full and adequate representation on the school council. In demographically complex communities, for example, all economic and ethnic groups should be represented. (See the description of the National Urban/Rural School Development in Joyce, Hersh, & McKibbin, 1983.)

Task 2: Develop relationships among the community, district administration, sources of technical assistance, and the council. It will take some time for the council to establish a process for studying the school, determining needs, establishing priorities, and developing a plan of action. At the outset community members on the council must establish a network of relationships throughout the community, to ensure efficient two-way communication. As the study proceeds, opinions and ideas should be solicited from and transmitted to the community. A considerable period of time will be needed to establish a network that will accomplish this comfortably and easily.

The council also needs to contact the school district administration to solicit its advice about educational goals for the community. Curriuculum guides and governance regulations should be assembled and examined. Relationships among the council, the district administration, and the board of education should be established. Generally speaking, school improvement councils can achieve wide latitude for themselves provided they do not violate board of education regulations. Also, central district offices periodically tend to initiate district-wide changes in certain aspects of the school program and these initiatives must be respected. If the school district is making a considerable effort in the area of science, for example, the council may simply want to facilitate that effort, developing its own initiatives in other areas. The exact relationship between councils and the central governance structure of the district will vary from situation to situation, and must be negotiated carefully and openly. The board of education and the district office should welcome the initiatives of the Responsible Parties, and, in turn, the Responsible Parties should welcome initiatives originating at the district level.

County, state, and federal guidelines can be ascertained through the district offices, as well as sources of funding for initiatives originating at those levels. For example, federal and state guidelines now mandate that handicapped students be provided the "least restricted education" available and provide resources to bring about certain changes. As this book is being written, there are considerable resources available in the area of special education, especially for teacher information and training.

Resources must be marshaled, however, and procedures established for obtaining them. Also, supervisors, higher education personnel, and technical assistants from county, state, and curriculum and teacher centers should be identified. The council may want to secure the services of a consultant to help them organize and learn to function effeciently. Evaluations of school-community councils such as the National Urban/Rural School Development Program have generally concluded that most councils can use considerable technical assistance, both in studying their school and implementing their plans. The council of the Responsible Parties must quickly learn a great deal about education in order to make informed decisions. Membership essentially constitutes an agreement to embark on a long course of study, and at many points in that course expert assistance will be needed and appreciated.

Task 3: Commence studying the school using the effectiveness criteria. The Responsible Parties now begin to study the school and its community. They aquaint themselves with the school program and how it is conducted. They interview teachers, community members, administrators, and children to ascertain what is going on and gather opinions about areas needing attention. They begin to draw a picture of the missions the school is currently fulfilling and the means being used to achieve them. What is our school like? What are the parts of its program like? What is it accomplishing? What might it accomplish?

The attributes described in the following questions provide a convenient tool for commencing the study of the school. The Responsible Parties can ask:

> Are the academic and social goals of the school clear to the community, students, faculty, and administrators?
>
> Is good order maintained? Is discipline consistent with the methods of the school?
>
> Is the school permeated with high expectations for student growth and achievement?
>
> Do the teachers feel efficacious?
>
> Is the climate caring and supportive? Do the students feel accepted and do they understand that the high expectations reflect the school's concern and caring for them?
>
> Is accomplishment publicly praised?
>
> Is administrative leadership clear, strong, and responsive?
>
> Does the community support education? Are parents involved?
>
> Are students busy with learning tasks that are appropriate to their learning abilities?
>
> Is progress monitored and are students kept informed about their development and achievement?
>
> Is the curriculum coherently organized?
>
> Is an appropriate variety of teaching strategies in use?
>
> Are there opportunities for students to share responsibility for the health of the school?

It is virtually certain that any organization of Responsible Parties that asks these questions will find ample opportunity to refine current practice and generate innovations.

Task 4: Select a focus for improvement. Gradually, a list of priorities develops and the task becomes one of deciding on an area of focus. Nearly everyone who studies a school using the effectiveness criteria finds numerous ways of improving it. When a council is just beginning, its best course is to begin with the effectiveness criteria and get Stage 1 (refinement) moving. Their attention can turn to curriculum areas and staff development in Stage 2 (renovation). Finally, fresh missions and means for accomplishing them can be explored in Stage 3 (redesign). As a council matures, continuous study by its members will create a situation where improvements have been implemented in some areas, while in others the debate is still raging about what to do and how to do it. Because it is easy to set too many goals and achieve none of them, a beginning council should always choose a specific focus — one on which there is relatively high agreement and for which procedures can be easily developed.

Task 5: Assemble the necessary resources. Once the focus is selected and the missions and means within that area have been identified, they should be communicated thoroughly to the community, the central district administration, and the teaching staff. The proposed change should be presented as an experimental attempt to improve education, one that will be modified as experience is accumulated, and which may be discarded if it proves ineffective. It is a serious mistake to present any proposed changes as a panacea to the problems of education. A modest approach that does not exaggerate the possibilities and that emphasizes the experimental nature of any innovation is the wiser course.

In addition, resources must be assembled and detailed plans made. If the area of improvement is the recruitment of volunteer aides, for example, the teachers must be surveyed to determine how aides can be used and what training will be necessary for them. The Responsible Parties need to advertise the positions and identify criteria for service. The process must be orderly, and a high level of communication is essential. If the objective is to make improvements in a curriculum area, guidelines for doing this must be established and the instructional materials brought together. Many great ideas for teaching are inadequately supported by a very thin base of materials. To succeed, curriculum planning must be backed up with the resources to make it work.

Task 6: Provide time for training. In probably every area worthy of change, people are required to learn some new behaviors. Curriculum changes require new teaching strategies and the mastery of new content by teachers and others. Changes in organization and in community relations require new kinds of conferences and counseling. Parents who volunteer to be aides find that they need skills in tutoring. The development of appropriate training and time for training is essential to successful innovation. One major reason that change has proved so difficult in many schools is simply that adequate personnel training has not been provided. At this point it is sufficient to point out that new skills must be identified and ways of learning them provided. In certain areas, consultants or university personnel will be needed. To omit training will virtually ensure failure. For many schools, this will be the first step in the development of regular substansive in-service training, and so it must lay the base for the more complex staff development required in Stages 2 and 3.

Task 7: Communicate, communicate, and communicate. Formal meetings should be held with community members, the teaching staff, and the district administration, to clarify what is going on and how objectives will be accomplished. All parties concerned need and have the right to know what is about to happen and why. Questions must be answered at this time and unanimity developed. Teachers and community members should enter the process with a friendly, supportive feeling of experimentation.

Task 8: Prepare the pilot study. At this point a plan should be developed for testing, evaluating, and revising selected elements of the innovation. It is important that representative elements of the innovation be tested because their effectiveness will vary according to the specific plan and setting in which they are used. If the change to be made is within a curriculum area, several teachers may volunteer to try out elements of the new procedures. The pilot can be developed through observation or an informal evaluation.

Task 9: Carry out the pilot study. Maximum support should be given to the individuals involved in testing elements of the innovation. Especially if new teaching strategies and content are involved, both teachers and students will be uncomfortable with the new material and procedures for some time; this discomfort should be expected.

Task 10: Revise the innovation. The pilot study almost surely will indicate the need for adjustments and perhaps for further training, which can occupy a considerable period of time depending on the complexity of the innovation. The pilot study will help determine the steps necessary to implement the change. The final plan for implementation can be generated at this time.

Task 11: Commence implementation. During this period a supportive social climate is most essential. Any change worth making involves new procedures that will be awkward at first. There will be a sense that things are not going as well as they were before, and for a time this will be true. For example, when volunteer aides are first brought into a school there generally is some feeling of chaos. The aides feel insecure and the teachers are uncertain how to employ them productively. This is a period of excitement combined with dismay. However, if the social climate is positive and all hands assist one another, the adjustment period is soon gotten through. A lengthy new curriculum should be implemented in stages, and training should continue throughout the early parts of implementation. It is extremely helpful if teachers can regularly share information about what is and is not working.

Task 12: Evaluate and fine tune the innovation. Over time, appropriate evaluation procedures should be used to find out how things are going. Further revisions usually will be necessary, and the need for such revisions should be taken in stride. Many innovations fail because the first implementation efforts are awkward and appear ineffective. Frequently the innovation is discarded at this point, when revision, adaptation, or further training would have been the better solution.

Evaluation should be planned into each part of the innovation to ensure that it is under continuous study. As the process of generating and implementing changes and evaluating their effects become established, the Responsible Parties will have a continuous flow of information that can be used for further decision making. On the basis of this information, effects should be made to fine tune the school program on a continuous basis.

STAGE 2

After several discrete innovations have been successfully made, Stage 2 (renovation) is ready to be launched. At this point the focus of the Responsible Parties shifts to major tasks such as the ones that follow:

1. Survey the curriculum areas and the overall social climate.
2. Clarify the goals for the area being studied.
3. Identify alternative means of accomplishing the goals.
4. Repeat Tasks 5 through 12 of Stage 1.

A brief look at the Stage 2 tasks is now in order.

Task 1: Survey the curriculum areas and the overall social climate. The major curriculum areas (science, mathematics, reading, etc.) come under scrutiny and at this point, the ones needing attention are selected. In addition to curriculum areas, improvement efforts might focus on matters such as these:

The social climate (developing a warm cooperative atmosphere)

School organization (developing teaching teams, etc.)

Community action programs (involving students in social service)

Developing additional personnel resources (obtaining and training volunteer teaching aides)

Securing and developing a continuing education program for adults (for example, communities into which Vietnamese refugees are moving are currently finding a considerable need in this area)

Even the basic skill areas (reading, writing and arithmetic) that receive considerable public attention are not easily brought into focus. Although teaching of basic skills is well established in most schools, it takes some time before the council can unravel the complexities of these programs and may develop a clear idea about directions for change. When a new school is being established, some attention must be given to all areas of study— a task of considerable complexity.

Task 2: Clarify the goals for the area being studied. The next step is to define just what the goals are of the area being studied. Most aspects of the school program contain possible competing missions and it is important to clarify these before the question of means is approached.

Task 3: Identify alternative means of accomplishing the goals. Once the goals have been identified the next task is to identify alternative ways of accomplishing them. In every curriculum area several alternatives exist. For example, changing the social climate of the school, or recruiting and training aides can both be accomplished in a variety of ways. For Task 3, the council probably can use the services of consultants in the areas under consideration.

Even the most experienced teachers generally are too busy to keep up with all the curriculum alternatives. At this point, the school improvement study must include not only the teachers representing the Responsible Parties but also respresentatives from or perhaps all of the teachers who would be involved in any change. Goals must be circulated and understood by both the community and the teaching staff. Furthermore, the teachers must help identify the alternative curriculum plans, materials, and teaching procedures that are needed to accomplish the curriculum goals. In this book I divide the means to an end into three categories: curricular — the organization of substance and teaching processes; technological — the assembly of materials and other instructional devices; and social — the organization of people and the development of a social climate appropriate to the mission.

Task 4: Repeat Tasks 5 through 12 of Stage 1. Repeat Task 5 through Task 12, in one curriculum area at a time. Several major innovations should not be inaugurated simultaneously, or the school will become unstable, but the school improvement process should become regular.

A Continuous Process

While one area of focus is receiving operational attention (Tasks 5 through 12 of Stage 1), examination of alternative missions and means (Tasks 1 through 3 of Stage 2) goes on in other areas. New focuses must be selected, resources organized, training commenced, pilot implementations undertaken, and full implementation developed. It is important to estimate how much improvement the school can manage at any one time and to search for an optimal level of change. Undertaking too much too quickly overtaxes the system, but undertaking too little too slowly does not provide adequate stimulation.

The Responsible Parties will eventually need standing committees to oversee major dimensions of the school program. These committees should engage in continuous review of their particular area and recommend changes. In addition, teachers and community members should be queried at regular intervals in order to identify areas needing attention.

The most efficient way to survey needs is probably through interviews with a sample of community members and teachers. These people should be asked to think about the school and its program, to contemplate the nature of the community, and to identify areas in need of change that are worth studying. As the community changes, new needs will emerge. Other needs can be identified by studying the children's attitudes and achievement. In addition, each standing committee should study the products of research and development in their areas. New developments in mathematics, reading, science, social studies, the arts, and so forth should be scrutinized, as well as new plans for organizing schools, training personnel, and so on. District offices, counties, states, and the federal government also will generate initiatives that should be examined by the Responsible Parties. Federal and state agencies support initiatives according to perceived social needs, which tend to vary among local school situations. The most effective councils look on these external initiatives as opportunities, and will select from the ones most appropriate to their school setting.

As part of their regular development program, teachers should attend conferences and search out materials and ideas in their fields. The Responsible Parties also will want to visit nearby schools and a few outside their immediate area to look for ideas that will be adaptable to their situation.

Clearly, embedding the school improvement process is essential. The first tentative moves will be uncomfortable to communities and schools that are not accustomed to the continuous change process. As time goes on, change will become more familiar, a positive social climate will develop, and community members and teachers will become comfortable working together. As each targeted improvement becomes embedded in the school, a general climate of receptivity to change and improvement will develop. School improvement will become normal rather than exceptional. Each effort lays the ground for the next . . . the next . . . and the next.

STAGE 3

At this stage we begin to consider the overall purpose of the school (its major missions) and rethink the entire structure of the school. The improvement process (selecting missions and the means to achieve them, assembling resources, and staff development) is the same at this stage as it was for Stage 2, but more intensive. The success of implementation efforts, however, will depend on past efforts to lay a base from which a thoroughgoing examination can proceed. The Jefferson school, described in Part II, is an example of a school that is in the Stage 3 state.

BUILDING RESISTANCE TO READY-MADE SOLUTIONS

We are able to distinguish a number of styles by which educational decisions traditionally have been made. One is the use of custom or tradition, which is more common than we sometimes realize.

Why, for example, do we have 12 grades in school? Is it because we have *always* had 12 grades? Why do so many schools begin in September and end in June? Is it because agrarian America of the nineteenth century needed the labor of the children in the fields during the summer? Why is history so often taught chronologically? Is it because history is best learned that way, or is it because events occurred that way? Why is American literature taught in the 11th grade and English literature in the 12th? Obviously, this is simply the way it has always been done.

The reason tradition is so attractive is that it provides ready-made solutions to questions that otherwise could become problems, and thus it simplifies the decision-making process. In daily living this is useful, even indispensable. The dangers are that a habitual or customary solution may rule our decisions long after such a solution has become outmoded and useless, or that we will come to rely on tradition to the point where we stop seeking creative solutions.

Another way to solve problems is to appeal to an expert or to some highly respected source. Should 5-year-olds be taught to read? We might ask a psychologist to give us an opinion. Should we have subject specialists in the primary school? Again, we might hope that authorities will tell us. We might ask a mathematician what mathematics should be taught in elementary school, or a businessman what high school curriculum is the best preparation for business.

We certainly should seek authoritative knowledge. Much uncertainty can be dissipated by listening to authority, and there are times when we must trust the judgment of the expert. But it is not wise simply to call in an authority and ask that person to be our decision maker. Educational knowledge rarely points to clear solutions that are appropriate for all situations. The authority should be consulted about the *options*, not asked to give us the answer.

Problems also can be solved by relying on common sense. The truth, in such cases, is "obvious," "self-evident," or "indisputable." We certainly want to rely on our good judgment, but we need to be suspicious of many commonsense ideas about education. Some obvious propositions have turned out to be quite wrong. For example, teachers once assumed that punishment extinguished poor responses — that punishing or correcting a child for misspelling a word would impel her or him to spell the word correctly thereafter. It has been found, however, that punishment often *reinforces* the original response; that is, it can fix the incorrect spelling in the learner's mind. Punishment also can create phobias, which turn the learner away from the subject matter.

Another commonsense solution to the problem of low achievement is to fail a child and keep him or her at the same grade level for another year. This procedure is also supposed to encourage the child to learn what he or she has failed to learn in the past. Yet nonpromotion actually may retard achievement; it has been found that unpromoted students tend to learn less than they would have if they had been promoted (Goodlad & Anderson, 1965).

Similarly, because common sense tells us that grouping children by ability facilitates learning, many schools and school districts employ homogeneous grouping. However, grouping by ability has not always proven to be an effective stimulant to learning and, in some cases, has retarded the achievement of the less able and has stigmatized some children. Segregating the handicapped seemed sensible to policy makers 30 years ago but is abhorrent today.

No easy antidote exists to the usual ways school programs come into existence, which is to let common practice dominate, to accept the solutions offered by one of two authorities, or to follow commonsense formulas. Schools in general are not as effective as they should be, precisely because easy, comfortable practices have been adopted without adequate thought or energy. It is difficult to improve schools because continuing current practice seems like the right thing to do. It would be much easier to institute better practice if teachers and community felt uneasy about the condition of their school. But in most cases, people accept the status quo and have trouble believing that the school actually can be made much better than it is.

If the Responsible Parties are to generate effective school improvement, they have to develop a systematic process for studying the school program. For most Responsible Parties, study of the school will generate a list of possible improvements to be made in the following areas:

Social Climate (Stage 1): For example, communicating goals to students, increasing a "can do" attitude, or establishing procedures for public acknowledgment of achievement

Technology (Stage 2): For example, adding microprocessors to the high school mathematics program

Curriculum (Stage 2): For example, overhauling the elementary school science and literature programs (most are quite poor)

Organization (Stage 3): For example, deploying some personnel to work in a microprocessing center or linking the school to broadcast courses

It is important to build gradually, to ensure that homeostatic reactions do not undermine the entire school improvement effort or prevent the formation of an effective working unit. Beginning at Stage 1 establishes the process and improves the climate of education. It is then possible to move to Stage 2, which establishes a process for improving the curriculum areas and embeds in the school the staff development necessary for curricular improvement. Finally, a matured school council can draw the entire community into the stimulating, difficult process of considering the overall direction of the school and bringing it into line with preferred missions (Stage 3).

Few Responsible Parties will want to overhaul the entire school at once — to proceed to Stage 3 without first going through Stages 1 or 2. To do so would exceed the capability of most communities to design, implement, or absorb change. However, if the school environment is continuously studied and small improvements are made regularly, it is reasonable to hope that an overall design can gradually be built, and that changes can be shaped so as to bring that design into existence over time. The school reform movements have left us a rich legacy of school models on which to build.

It is important to remember that school improvement is a process that should never cease. We can't get away cheap — it's not enough to study the school every 20 years, make a few changes, and then let it roll along for 2 more decades. The process of school improvement must be built carefully and then be made permanent.

10

The Role of School Districts and Federal and State Initiatives

Program improvement must be a part of the ongoing life of every school. The school is the unit of education in our society and we citizens like to be involved with our schools. We can't make a school better through legislation or regulation, by testing or by complaining. What we *can* do is to infect all the units of the system with the spirit and procedures that will guarantee ongoing improvement efforts.

School districts and state and federal agencies have important roles to play. They can generate initiatives for school improvement and can provide an organizational context, support services, and research and development efforts that may be very important to the improvement of local schools. However, the health of each of our schools will finally determine the quality of education for the students served by that school, and each school has to have the capability to generate initiatives and to deal responsibly and vigorously with innovations that come from outside of it. The most important role that district offices, state governments and departments of education, and the federal government can play is to help schools develop that capability.

DISTRICTS

Districts vary so greatly in the United States — they range in size from one tiny school to the massive New York City system with more than 60,000 teachers — that we sometimes wonder whether the word has operational meaning. Managing the massive logistics of the larger districts involves many operations that simply are not needed in the smaller arenas.

When it comes to the improvement of curriculum and instruction, however, many of the same objectives need to be accomplished in all districts, and the means for accomplishing them have structural similarities despite the differing complexity of the settings. For small districts to assemble sufficient resources to approach many tasks, small districts must pool their resources and draw on intermediate agencies such as regional service centers, county offices of education, and universities. These districts need not be discouraged about resources. Recent surveys (Joyce, Bush, and McKibbin, 1981) indicate that active small rural districts provide as much in-service education and clinical support to their schools as do the large districts or the wealthy suburban ones — the commitment of the district leadership is what makes the difference, not the district's demographic composition. The problem for large districts is the opposite of the problem smaller districts face. Large districts must break down their organization into smaller units or families of schools, so that the improvement process does not become too administratively unwieldy.

Whether their districts are large or small, district organizers can contribute to school improvement in several significant ways. First, it is critically important that building administrators and team leaders or lead teachers receive up-to-date leadership training, which includes training to organize school committees of Responsible Parties and lead them through the process described in this book, or equivalent processes. Leadership training also includes the study of curricular and instructional alternatives and contemporary educational technologies. Also necessary, and closely related, is training in organizational development — how to build an effective, supportive problem-solving faculty group. Unfortunately, much past administrative training has not included these elements, so most personnel now in service need extensive programs of study.* Not much will happen without effective leadership. Each school needs a team of trained leaders, including teachers.

Second, the district leadership must ensure that a group of Responsible Parties is established and that the process of school improvement begins.

Third, the district must provide both resources and personnel who carry out extensive staff development. Although a district (or a coalition of small districts) can draw on consultants from universities and intermediate agencies, districts (or subsections of large districts) must develop their own cadres of trainers who can help their colleagues study teaching and assist them in the curriculum implementation process. The cadres can consist of teams of teachers drawn from schools in the one area — a cluster of about a dozen schools is feasible — with each school contributing several members to the cadre. Once established and trained, the district cadres can offer service to the school faculties in their area.

Fourth, the district leadership team must ensure that the building-level leaders and the cadres have access to information about promising avenues for school improvement. For example, the microprocessor is currently receiving much attention as a learning device. Some districts and schools have developed very effective ways of using them. Information about successful uses of microprocessors in those schools can be used by other schools to design effective utilization in their own settings.

Finally, districts must contribute what is almost spiritual leadership. This contributes to the creation of a community of schools that believe they can deliver education of the best quality to their students and strive to become ever better. We have learned from recent studies that effective organizations in other domains — business, industry, and athletics — maintain high quality by never becoming complacent. Whether it is the Dallas Cowboys or Hewlett-Packard or our neighborhood school, that part of the story is the same.

---

*For greater detail see Joyce, Hersh, and McKibbin (1983).

STATES

The role of the states in relation to districts resembles the role of the districts in relation to the schools: the states must ensure that the district leadership is well trained for the roles described in the previous section. Training for many superintendents and supervisors, as for principals and teachers, has not included school improvement as a central focus. The states need to strengthen their intermediate units and university faculties of education to increase their ability to provide needed services to the districts. Again, this kind of preparation is needed for all personnel.

It is very important that states survey the entire scene and initiate improvements in particular directions. When they do so, however, they need to provide research, development, and training resources, so that their initiative can become a real force in the education of the children and not simply a mandate. For example, many states are now encouraging (or mandating) the use of microproccesors and providing resources to schools to purchase them, but they are not providing adequate funding for research to determine how best to use the devices, and they are not providing adequate training for school personnel. Mainstreaming of students with learning handicaps is another example. Both federal and state governments have legislated it and approved resources for teachers, but many schools have not been able to figure out how to mainstream productively. Thus, in many schools, the letter of the law has been observed but not the spirit of it, and what should have been a productive innovation is not working in many schools because adequate development work and training was not carried out. Personally, I am strongly in favor of mainstreaming but am sickened by what has happened in many places. (Again, see Joyce et al., *The Structure of School Improvement,* for greater detail, and consult the national evaluation by SRI International.)

States could do much more than they have to provide research and development monies. They also should make much more effective use of universities and the staffs of the larger districts to ensure that a steady supply of fresh ideas comes forth and that these ideas are accompanied by the development work that is needed to make them practical.

THE FEDERAL GOVERNMENT

I will not deal here with general questions about the federal role in education, but will confine discussion to the role of the federal government in the school improvement process. There are three critical areas:

First, it is important for the federal government, as for the districts and the states, to provide necessary components when initiatives are made. The federal record ranges from very good to very poor. For example, when Congress became concerned about the education of teachers for poor and minority children, it was clear that the system for teacher preparation needed a boost in that direction, and thus the National Teacher Corps was established. The federal government went far beyond the "Here's some money, now do it" approach. It established a fine organization that united schools and universities in the effort, created recruitment centers, and provided for development and excellent training of both district teachers and university-level teacher educators. At the other extreme, however, the lack of development and training has made the mainstreaming effort much less effective than it should be. Because some districts were ready and others weren't, too little was done to implement mainstreaming; bilingual education similarly suffers for lack of development and training resources.

Second, the federal government is in a unique position to support research and development pertaining to schools and to the preparation of teachers and educational leaders. The federal government also can ensure that research and development are balanced. For example, currently there is interest in educational technology, and investment in this area is badly needed, but support to the humanities and social studies should not cease as a result. Universities, districts, and regional research and development centers need a continuing and balanced funding program to ensure that research in important areas of education does not languish.

Finally, the federal arena should be a model for the national dialogue about educational objectives and how to achieve them. Finger-pointing and quick and dirty solutions have no place at that level. Although crash programs will not change large social institutions in an enduring way, affirmative leadership can accomplish a great deal in a remarkably short period of time. The education system in the United States is not a large corporation, but rather, as I said earlier, a collection of 17,000 separate school districts. Thus we will not have a Lee Iacocca to reorganize its finances, its research and development program, or its delivery. We can have the same spirit, however, and if it is radiated from the federal level, it will infuse the state and local levels as well. Schools are an investment in people. School improvement depends on an investment in the people who teach, and those who create educational ideas and develop them until they are practical. We must be simultaneously hard-headed and high-spirited about this. Our investment is realized only in part through the provision of material resources. Moral energy is also needed. Believing we can have a wonderful education for our children will help it come true.

References

Adler, M. (1982). *The Paideia proposal.* New York: Macmillan.

Berman, P., & McLaughlin, M. (1975). *Federal programs supporting educational change:* 1. Santa Monica, CA: Rand Corporation.

Cremin, L. (1965). *The genius of American education.* Pittsburgh, PA: University of Pittsburgh Press.

Dewey, J. (1918). *Democracy and education.* New York: Macmillan.

Fullan, M. (1983). *The meaning of educational change.* Toronto: Ontario Institute for Studies in Education.

Fullan, M., & Pomfret, A. (1977). Research on curriculum and instructional innovation. *Review of Educational Research, 47*(1), pp. 335-397.

Goodlad, J. (1983). *A place called school.* New York: McGraw-Hill.

Goodlad, J., & Anderson, R. (1965). *The nongraded elementary school.* New York: Harcourt, Brace and Jovanovitch.

Goodlad, J., & Klein, F. (1970). *Looking behind the classroom door.* Worthington, OH: Charles E. Jones.

Gordon, W. (1961). *Synectics.* New York: Harper & Row.

Hall, G. E., & Loucks, S. (1977). A developmental model for determining whether the treatment is actually implemented. *American Educational Research Journal, 14*(3), pp. 263-276.

Joyce, B., Bush, R., & McKibbin, M. (1981). *The California staff development study.* Palo Alto, CA: Booksend Laboratories.

Joyce, B., Hersh, R., & McKibbin, M. (1983). *The structure of school improvement.* White Plains, NY: Longman.

Joyce, B., & Morine, G. G. (1976). *Creating the school.* Boston, MA: Little, Brown.

Joyce, B., & Showers, B. (1983). *Power in staff development through research on training.* Association for Supervision and Curriculum Development. Washington, DC.

Joyce, B., Showers, B., Dalton, M., & Beaton, C. (1985). *The search for validated skills of teaching: Four lines of inquiry.* Paper presented to the Annual Meeting of the American Educational Research Association, Chicago, IL.

Joyce, B., & Weil, M. (1980). *Models of teaching.* Englewood Cliffs, NJ: Prentice-Hall.

National Commission on Excellence in Education. (Bell; 1984). *A Nation at risk: The full account.* Edited by USA Research.

Showers, B. (1985). Teachers coaching teachers: The dynamics of staff development. *Educational Leadership, 42(7),* pp. 43-48.

Sizer, T. (1984). *Horace's compromise — the dilemma of the American high school.* Boston, MA: Houghton Mifflin.

Slavin, R. (1982). *Cooperative learning.* White Plains, NY: Longman.

Smith, L., & Keith, P. (1971). *Anatomy of an innovation.* New York: Wiley.

Spaulding, R. (1970). *EIP.* Durham, NC: Duke University Press.

SRI International. *Evaluation of the implementation of public law 94-142.* Menlo Park, CA: SRI International.

Walberg, H. (1985). *Why Japanese productivity excels.* Paper presented to the Annual Meeting of the American Educational Research Association, Chicago.

Bibliography

Improving America's Schools is designed to present an argument about school improvement and how it might be conducted. The school improvement process is complex and to study it thoroughly requires many references. In the following few pages a number of the more important books and articles are briefly annotated as a guide to the study of the field of innovation in education. These items are in addition to the references, which you might want to consult as well. The recent "national reports" should be read in the original. Michael Fullan's *The Meaning of Educational Change* is very important, possibly the key to the field. *The Structure of School Improvement* (Joyce, Hersh, & McKibbin) is the "parent" of *Improving America's Schools* and is a much more comprehensive treatment of the school improvement process.

Apple, M. (1979). *Ideology and curriculum.* London: Routledge and Kegan Paul.
    A serious philisophical analysis of the value orientations that are explicit and tacit in curriculums.

Argyris, C., & Schon, E. (1974). *Theory into practice: Increasing professional effectiveness.* San Francisco: Jossey-Bass.
    A theoretical and practical guide to behavior in organizations.

Baldridge, J., & Deal, T. (1975). *Managing change in educational organizations.* Berkeley: McCutchan.
    A careful analysis of the executive role in educational organizations as they exist and as they might be.

Ball, S., & Bogatz, G. A. (1970). *The first year of Sesame Street.* Princeton, NJ: Educational Testing Service.
    Although chiefly a report on the effectiveness of the famous educational television program, the analysis is worthwhile reading for anyone who wants to know how to create and implement an educational innovation and the dynamics that make one effective.

Bates, T. (1980). Applying new technology to distance education: A case study from the Open University. *Educational Broadcasting International, 13*(3), 110-114.

    The Open University has been a major innovation and on a nationwide scale. It has used unusual combinations of technology and organization to deliver high-quality education to a massive number of people. Learning how it works yields knowledge about how much smaller-scale innovations can take place.

Becker, W. C. (1977). Teaching reading and language to the disadvantaged —What we have learned from field research. *Harvard Educational Review, 47,* 518-543.

    Becker and his associates have developed, implemented, and evaluated a large-scale instructional system for teaching the basic skills in elementary schools. Their knowledge about how to engineer and implement curriculum systems is of interest both for what it says about the existence of effective educational technologies and also for the organizational care and staff development effort that make an innovation translate into different settings.

Berman, P., & McLaughlin, M. (1975). *Federal programs supporting educational change.* Santa Monica, CA: Rand Corporation.

    An exceedingly careful analysis of a number of federal programs in a variety of communities. Concludes with the identification of factors that influenced the implementation of those programs and thus gave them the opportunity to have an impact on student learning.

Brookover, W., et al. (1977). *Schools can make a difference.* East Lansing: Michigan State University, College of Urban Development.

    One of the major studies attempting to identify the characteristics of schools that generate more-than-average student achievement. Should be read in the original. The many summaries of the characteristics of effective schools can oversimplify the dynamic that appears to work.

Brophy, J. *Teacher stimulation of student motivation to learn.* Paper presented to the annual meeting of the American Educational Research Association, Chicago.

    Brophy has been one of the leaders in the study of unusually effective teachers. This study is just one of the many he has done and is a good beginning for one who wants to know more about the findings from research on effective teachers and how such research is conducted.

Chamberlin, C., & Chamberlin, E. (1943). *Did they succeed in college?* New York: Harper & Row.

    The classic study of the Progressive Schools movement. Of interest to anyone interested in the school as a unit of change. Should give pause to anyone who believes casual rumors that the Progressive movement was bad for the academic health of its students.

Charters, W.W., Jr., & Pellegrin, R. (1973). Barriers to the innovation process: Four case studies of differentiated staffing. *Administrative Science Quarterly, 1*, 3-14.

The authors provide a realistic analysis of the problems that typically plague innovations, problems that occur in nearly every setting. A clear message that we cannot make the school setting congenial to innovations without making some major changes in it.

Clark, D., & Guba, E. (1977). *A study of teacher education institutions as innovators, knowledge producers, and change agents.* Bloomington, IN: Indiana University.

The definitive study of faculties of teacher education as settings for knowledge production and innovation. Higher education conditions that promote innovation in higher education are strikingly similar to those that facilitate innovation in schools.

Crandall, D.P., & Associates. (1983). *People, policies, and practices: Examining the chain of school improvement.* Andover, MA: The Network.

A multidimensional study of innovation in a variety of school settings. The analysis speaks to the nature of the setting, the personnel, the training given, and the innovation itself, as these factors contribute to the likelihood that an innovation will take root and have a chance to do its work.

Doyle, W., & Ponder, G. (1977-1978). The practicality ethic in teacher decision making. *Interchange, 8*, 1-12.

An analysis of the way educators think as they make decisions. Directly informs the problem of bringing people together around unifying ideas in a setting where the day-to-day dominates.

Eisner, E. (1979). *The educational imagination: On the design and evaluation of school programs.* New York: Macmillan.

A long view of the possibilities of education in our society. To be read whenever one begins to succumb to short-run, "quick bottom-line," narrow-gauge thinking.

Freire, P. (1970). *The pedagogy of the oppressed.* New York: Herder and Herder.

A very thoughtful "anti-establishment" view of schools and schooling. Sensitizes us to the serious and negative impact schooling can have on people's lives. Written with revolutionary fervor.

Fullan, M., & Park, P. (1980). *Curriculum implementation: A resource guide.* Toronto: Ontario Institute for studies in education.

The governmental agency of a major Canadian province commissioned these scholars of educational change to create a document that could be used as a basis for the planning of policy and operations. Illustrates the kind of relationship that can be developed between research and policy planning.

Gold, B. A., & Miles, M. (1981). *Whose school is it anyway? Parent-teacher conflict over an innovative school.* New York: Praeger.

124 / Bibliography

The parents must be partners with the school if an innovation is to work. Creating and maintaining that partnership is tricky and demanding, as this fascinating case study reveals.

Goodlad, J., & Klein, F. (1970). *Looking behind the classroom door.* Worthington, OH: Charles E. Jones.

A thoughtful analysis of what happened to the innovations of the sixties and why. A sober documentation of the intractability of the present organization of the school and the classroom.

Goodlad, J. (1983). *A place called school.* New York: McGraw-Hill.

Goodlad's suggestions for reform. Argues for a restructuring of the community of teachers and students.

Greene, M. (1973). *Teacher as stranger.* New York: Teachers College Press.

A fascinating perspective on the problem of the achievement of personal and professional meaning in teaching.

Hall, G., & Loucks, S. (1977). A developmental model for determining whether the treatment is actually implemented. *American Educational Research Journal, 14*(3), 263-276.

The most widely used framework for studying the implementation of innovations. Makes distinctions between levels of mastery and understanding that enable us to predict whether an innovation will persist.

House, E. (1981). Three perspectives on innovation: Technological, cultural, and political. In R. Lehming and M. Kane (Eds.), *Improving schools: Using what we know* (pp. 13-34). Beverly Hills, CA: Sage.

Discusses three general types of approach to innovation. These may also be seen as dimensions of the innovative process.

Howey, K. (1980). *Successful school practices: Perceptions of a total school faculty.* San Francisco: Far West Laboratory for Educational Research and Development.

An insightful look at the views of teachers about schools and schooling. An important document for those who wish to compare the emic and etic views of the educational process.

Joyce, B. (Ed.). (1978). *Involvement: A study of the shared governance of education.* Washington, DC: The Eric Clearinghouse on Teacher Education.

The story of the Urban-Rural School Development Program, in which school-community councils governed the school improvement process in 26 poverty-stricken communities. The data underlie the central thesis of *Improving America's Schools.*

Joyce. B., Bush, R., & McKibbin, M. (1981). *The California staff development study: The compact report.* Sacramento: California State Department of Education.

Reports a study of staff development received by more than 2,000 California teachers in a variety of settings. Details the weakness of the staff development system in one of the nation's most active states. Sets forth a program for reorganizing the system.

Lortie, D. (1975). *Schoolteacher.* Chicago: The University of Chicago Press.
The classic study of the ethos of teaching. The clearest definition of the workplace and why it persists as it does in the midst of other social changes.

McKibbin, M., & Joyce, B. Psychological states and staff development. *Theory into practice 19*(4), 248-255.
A study of the self-concepts of teachers as factors in their response to innovations.

Mertens, S., & Yarger, S. *Teacher centers in action.* Syracuse, NY: Syracuse Area Teacher Center.
The study of federally funded, teacher-governed centers for staff development. A careful analysis of what changes teacher involvement did and did not bring about in the content and process of in-service education.

Miles, M. (1981). Mapping the common properties of schools. In R. Lehming and M. Kane (Eds.), *Improving schools: Using what we know* (pp. 170-209). Beverly Hills, CA: Sage.
An imaginative description of the internal dynamic in and the relationship between the internal and external human systems of the schools. A concise summary of a very complex literature.

Rhine, W. R. (Ed.). (1981). *Making schools more effective: New directions from follow through.* New York: Academic Press.
Follow Through was a massive attempt at school improvement for young children. The experience of the effort is accumulated here in a most candid series of essays.

Sarason, S. (1972). *The creation of settings and the future societies.* San Francisco: Jossey-Bass.
A general treatise on the problem of change and human meaning, by the author of *The culture of the school.*

Schaefer. R. (1967). *The school as a center of inquiry.* New York: Harper & Row.
A powerful description of the school as a community of teachers who continually study the efforts of teaching on learning. A clear statement of the conditions that make team teaching personally and professionally rewarding and, by implication, what was missing when it did not work.

Schmuck, R., Runkel, P., Arends, J., & Arends, R. (1978). *The second handbook of organizational development in schools.* Palo Alto, CA: Mayfield Press.

The accumulation of experience from the attempts to change the organizational climate of schools.

Shane, H. (1977). *Curriculum change: Toward the 21st century.* Washington, DC: National Education Association.

Perspectives on the future. The school will have to change. How can the direction of change be shaped to take the best advantage of technology and social changes?

Smith, L., & Keith, P. (1971). *Anatomy of educational innovation.* New York: Wiley.

A case study of an innovative school, which has become one of the classic ethnographies of an attempt to radically change a school. The analysis is a forecast of a science of innovation, grounded as it is in the theory of social, psychological, and organizational behavior.

Wilson, C. (1971). *The open-access curriculum.* Boston: Allyn & Bacon.

A fine blueprint for a school that vigorously tends to the academic, personal, and social needs of students.

Zaltman, G., Duncan, R., & Holbeck, J. (1973). *Innovation and organizations.* New York: Wiley.

A thorough analysis of the processes by which organizational stability can be preserved in organizations that prize innovation. Makes clear that innovation and stability are not adversaries, but necessary for each other.

Index